Happy Birth[day]

Look forward [to getting]
quizzed on some of this.

Have a good one.

Chris, Sophie

& Cecily.

A

Tyne

&

Northu

Misc

Zymurgy

A CIP catalogue record for this book is available from the
British Library

Cover design by Nick Ridley

10 9 8 7 6 5 4 3 2 1

Printed and bound by Clowes Limited, Suffolk, U.K.

ISBN 1 903506 107

Published by Zymurgy Publishing, Newcastle upon Tyne
© 2004 Zymurgy Publishing

Acknowledgements & Thanks

Andrew Smith for suggesting the idea in the first place.

Many books have been an invaluable source of information. A number of books have particularly useful; The Millennium History of the North East of England by David Simpson, The River Tyne From Sea to Source by Ron Thornton, Natural North by Allan Potts and numerous books published by Frank Graham

Graham Anderson, Alan Baxter, Shirley Brown and BASIS, Michael Byrne, John Clayson, Mel Deighton, Bryan Ellis, Alan Grint, Holly, Hoults Estate (everyone who works there), John Jobling, Gary Kidd, Steve Ingham, Ray Marshall, Sheyl Muxworthy, Nick Ridley, Robert Rowell, Charlotte Sly, Amanda Thomas, Kathy Wilcox and the Newcastle-Gateshead Initiative.

The Local Studies Section of Newcastle City Library has been invaluable, the Patents Office has also been most helpful. Tyne and Wear Museums have been a great source of information. Local media; City Life, Evening Chronicle, The Journal and listeners to BBC Radio Newcastle Blue Bus programme.

Internet sites have been useful, in particular for checking the accuracy of information.

One last invaluable source of information needs to be credited, people down the pub!

Introduction

The aim of *A Tyneside and Northumberland Miscellany* is to celebrate the area and its people. A number of people included were born in the region and achieved 'greatness' outside the region, some have been welcomed from elsewhere in the country or indeed the world. Many people listed were born in Tyneside or Northumberland and their life's work has taken place locally.

It has been necessary to be brief and highly selective. Hopefully entries will whet the readers appetite and will be the starting point for further reading.

Contents

Geography

Geology

Geology has had a critical role in the development of the region.

Silurian Period

During the Silurian period, 450 million years ago, Northumberland was far south of the equator jammed between two continents. Volcanic activity followed 50 million years later producing lava and ash, creating the Cheviot Hills. Around 350 million years ago, at the start of the Carboniferous period, Northumberland had moved closer to the equator and was submerged by a tropical sea.

Carboniferous Period

Over the 60 million years of the Carboniferous period, rivers brought sand and mud which is now shale and sandstone. Decaying trees, ferns and other plant life were compressed by the sand and mud to produce the coal that stimulated the industrial growth of the region millions of years later. Earth movements in the late Carboniferous period tilted and moved rock formations towards the east and south. Magma came from deep down within the earth's crust to infill between layers of sedimentary rock.

The Great Whin Sill

On cooling, the molten rock crystallized forming dolerite; a hard black rock that makes up the Great Whin Sill. This hard rock forms: the Farne Islands, the cliffs on which Bamburgh and Dunstanburgh castles are built and the land on which the central section of Hadrian's Wall is constructed.

The Ice Age

The last key stage in geological development started 2.5 million years ago, when global cooling led to ice sheets across the county. Ice scoured the landscape and left glacial deposits, resulting in boulder clay that can be seen on a number of coastal cliffs to this day. At the end of the Ice Age about 10,000 years ago, sea levels rose driving people inland.

Relief

Coastal Plane

East of the Great North Road is mainly a coastal plain of intensively farmed rich and fertile arable land.

The Cheviots

The north of the county is dominated by the Cheviot Hills; round topped, poorly drained and boggy. Often difficult terrain for walkers, the Cheviot is the final challenge on the Pennine Way.

Simonside Hills

The Simonside Hills are Northumberland's second hill range, not as high but more rugged than the Cheviots with sandstone outcrops. South of Rothbury in Coquetdale is excellent country for walking.

Tynedale and Hexhamshire

The south of the county is dominated by the Tyne Valley and its beautiful rolling countryside. There are a number of steep hills in Hexhamshire.

Haltwhistle, the centre of Britain, is surrounded by undulating upland.

20 High Points

Name	Height
The Cheviot	2,675 ft
Hedgehope Hill	2,348 ft
Auchope Cairn	2,332 ft
Windy Gyle	2,032 ft
Cuchat Law	2,020 ft
Bloodybush Edge	2,001 ft
The Shiel	1,985 ft
Peel Fell	1,975 ft
The Curr	1,849 ft
Beefstand Hill	1,842 ft
Thirl Moor	1,829 ft
Wool Meath	1,809 ft
Limestone Knowe	1,801 ft
Scald Hill	1,797 ft
Newton Tors	1,762 ft
Catcleuch Shin	1,742 ft
Ravens Knowe	1,729 ft
Shilhope Law	1,644 ft
Tosson Hill	1,444 ft
Simonside Hills	1,408 ft

Principal Rivers

The Tweed

This famous salmon fishing river is mainly an English river but, apart from the Till, its main tributaries are Scottish. The Tweed rises in lush rolling countryside beneath the peaks of the Cheviots. At the tiny hamlet of Carham it forms the border between Northumberland and Scotland. The Tweed passes through the Scottish towns of Kelso and Coldstream and north of the remains of Norham Castle before passing under Robert Stephenson's 28 arch Royal Border Bridge at Berwick upon Tweed. Berwick is on the north bank and Tweedmouth on the south bank.

The Aln

Rises near Alnham, passes through Alnwick (the town that *Country Life* considered to be the best place to live in Britain) and Lesbury before reaching the sea at Almouth.

The Coquet

Rises in the Outer Golden Pot in wild Thirllmoor country. At Linsheels it is joined by Ushaw Burn which flows from the Cheviot. The Coquet passes through Rothbury and past Brinkburn Priory before reaching the sea at Amble. In Amble there is a traditional harbour and the largest modern marina in Northumberland.

The Wansbeck

The name is probably due to the huge rocks near its source known as the Wannys: Great Wanny, Little Wanny, Aird Law and Hepple Heaugh - hence Wannys Beck has become Wansbeck. It passes many famous Northumberland sites: Wallington, Middleton Hall, Mitford, Morpeth and Bothal before reaching the sea at Cambois Bay.

The Blyth

At Belsay it is a pretty river, at Ponteland it is joined by the river Pont and its short course of 20 miles ends at Blyth. The Port of Blyth is domimated by wind turbines including Britain's first offshore wind turbines that can produce up to 2MW each. The port handles more than 1,000,000 tonnes of cargo a year.

The Tyne

Fed by north and south flowing tributaries.

The North Tyne starts beyond Kielder at the western limits of the Cheviot Hills, on the lower slopes of Peel Fell on a plain known as Deadwater Fell. It flows into Europe's largest man-made lake, Kielder Water. It passes through Bellingham, is joined by the Rede at Redesmouth, flowing past Chollerford and Wall to the Meeting of the Waters.

The South Tyne rises on Cross Fell just outside Northumberland in Cumbria, enters Northumberland at Slaggyford under the magnificent Lambley Viaduct, then through Haltwhistle, Bardon Mill and Haydon Bridge before joining the North Tyne.

The Meeting of the Waters occurs just before Hexham. The course of the Tyne then flows past Corbridge, Riding Mill, Ovingham, Prudhoe and Wylam before reaching Tyneside at Newburn.

Through urban Tyneside on the north bank it passes Lemington, Scotswood, Elswick, Newcastle Quayside, the Ouseburn, St Peters, Walker Shore, Wallsend, Willington Quay, North Shields and reaches the sea at Tynemouth. On the south bank it passes Blaydon, Derwent Haugh, The Metro Centre, Dunston, Low Team, Gateshead Quayside, Felling Shore, Bill Quay, Hebburn, Jarrow, Tyne Dock and reaches the sea at South Shields.

The Tyne is now the best river to catch salmon by the rod in Britain.

Local Government

Northumberland County Council is split into seven districts: Alnwick, Berwick, Blyth, Castle Morpeth, Tynedale and Wansbeck. Tyneside is made up of four local authorities: Gateshead, Newcastle, North Tyneside and South Tyneside.

It is estimated that there are five times as many sheep as people living in Northumberland.

Council Name

Alnwick District Council . . . .

Berwick upon Tweed District Council . . . .

Blyth Valley Borough Council . . . .

Castle Morpeth District Council . . . .

Gateshead Metropolitan Borough Council . . . .

Newcastle upon Tyne City Council . . . .

North Tyneside Metropolitan Borough Council . . . . .

Northumberland County Council . . . .

South Tyneside Metropolitan Borough Council . . . . . .

Tynedale District Council . . . .

Wansbeck District Council . . . .

Administrative Base	Population	Area (sq km)	Density (per sq km)
. . Alnwick	31,355	1,080	29
. . Berwick Upon Tweed	26,132	972	27
. . Seaton Deleval	81,611	70	1,160
. . Morpeth	49,043	619	79
. . Gateshead	190,694	142	1,340
. . Newcastle	260,268	113	2,294
. . Wallsend	191,255	82	2,321
. . Morpeth	308,386	5,013	62
. . South Shields	152,340	64	2,365
. . Hexham	59,200	2,219	27
. . Ashington	61,045	67	914

Reverse Telephone Directory

This directory is based on the long established British Telecom numbering system and does not include numbers belonging to cable operators. The first location is the exchange as listed by Oftel, the Office of Telecommunications. More recent number allocations are difficult to be geographically specific and are therefore excluded.

01289	Berwick upon Tweed
01434 (6)	Hexham
01434 (3)	Haltwhistle
01434 (2)	Bellingham
01661	Prudhoe, Belsay, Ponteland, Stamfordham, Wylam
01665	Alnwick, Alnmouth, Chathill, Embleton, Longhoughton, Powburn, Shilbottle
01668	Bamburgh, Wooler
01669	Rothbury
01670	Morpeth, Bedlington, Blyth, Cramlington, Felton, Scots Gap, Stannington
01830	Kirkwhelpington, Otterburn
0191	Tyneside
232	Newcastle City Centre, Shieldfield, Ouseburn
236	Wideopen
237	New Hartley, Seaton Delaval, Seghill
251	Whitley Bay
252	Whitley Bay

253	Monkseaton, Shiremoor,
257	North Shields
258	North Shields
259	North Shields
261	Newcastle City Centre
262	Walker, Wallsend
264	West Denton
265	Byker, Heaton
266	High Heaton, Longbenton
267	Chapel House, Lemington, Newburn, Throckley, Walbottle
268	Killingworth
273	Benwell, Elswick
274	Fenham
276	Ouseburn, Walkergate
281	Jesmond
284	Gosforth
285	Gosforth, Kenton
286	Westerhope
296	North Shields
410	Ouston
413	Ryton
414	Blaydon, Winlaton Mill
420	Whickham
421	Hebburn, Lobley Hill
427	South Shields
428	Jarrow
451	Hebburn, Jarrow
454	South Shields

Postal Code Areas

NE1 Newcastle City Centre
NE2 Jesmond
NE3 Gosforth
NE4 Newcastle West City
NE5 Kenton
NE6 Heaton, Byker
NE7 High Heaton
NE8 Gateshead Centre
NE9 Gateshead South
NE10 Gateshead West
NE11 East Gateshead
NE12 Killingworth
NE13 Seaton Burn
NE15 Newcastle - outer West
NE16 Swalwell
NE17 Chopwell
NE18 Stamfordham
NE19 Otterburn
NE20 Ponteland
NE21 Blaydon
NE22 Bedlington
NE23 Cramlington
NE24 Blyth
NE25 Seaton Delaval
NE26 Whitley Bay
NE27 Shiremoor
NE28 Wallsend
NE29 North Shields
NE30 Tynemouth
NE31 Hebburn

NE32 Jarrow
NE33 South Shields (north)
NE34 South Shields (south)
NE35, 36, 37 and 38 are not in Tyneside
NE39 High Spen
NE40 Ryton
NE41 Crawcrook
NE42 Prudhoe
NE43 Stocksfield
NE44 Riding Mill
NE45 Corbridge
NE46 Hexham
NE47 Haydon Bridge
NE48 Wark
NE49 Haltwhistle
NE61 Morpeth
NE62 Choppington
NE63 Ashington
NE64 Newbiggin-by-the-Sea
NE65 Amble
NE66 Alnwick
NE67 Chathill
NE68 Seahouses
NE69 Bamburgh
NE70 Belford
NE71 Wooler
TD15 Berwick upon Tweed

History

A Brief History of Tyneside & Northumberland

Pre-history

The region was uninhabited 5,000 years ago.

It was first populated by Mesolithic people, who were later succeeded by Neolithic people. The region was then invaded by Beaker (Bronze Age) people 4,000 years ago

The Romans

The Romans arrived in the 1st century and stayed until the end of the 4th century. It was the northern outpost of the Roman Empire when Emperor Hadrian commissioned the building of the wall that is named after him. Hadrian who is believed to have been the only bearded Roman emperor, never saw the wall completed. It is estimated that the wall was constructed from 3.7 million tonnes of stone. Hadrian's Wall is a world heritage site.

Writing tablets found at Vindolanda are considered by the British Museum to be the most prized items in their collection. One of the tablets informs a soldier that clean underwear has been sent.

Anglo-Saxon

In 620 AD the Anglo-Saxon Kingdom of Northumbria was established. 15 years later the King of Northumbria regained leadership of the Anglo-Saxons, but only for 20 or so years.

By the end of the 9th century Viking raids into Northumbria had started and Norsemen controlled the region until the end of the 10th century.

The Normans

The famous date of 1066 and the Norman Conquest led to changes. Newcastle's strategic position led to the building of the 'New Castle' in 1080 by Robert, the son of William I. It was during this period that many castles were built. Northumberland has more castles than any other county.

The Middle Ages

Newcastle grew and became an important medieval trading centre - wool being the most important commodity. The export of coal to London and other ports had become established by the end of the 14th century, the trade growing rapidly between 1566 and 1625 (a 12-fold growth).

In rural Northumberland towards the end of the 16th century 'reiving' was a major problem involving clans from both sides of the border. The raiders would steal, kidnap, destroy property and murder. This was by no means a new problem, raiders had come from Scotland for hundreds of years.

The 18th Century

The 18th century and the Georgian era were periods of rapid urban development, fortunately we can still enjoy Georgian architecture today.

The 19th Century

Tyneside and Northumberland was arguably the birthplace of the industrial revolution and manufacturing. The history and development of the region is linked to coal, railways, shipping and shipbuilding.

Major Roman Sites

There are Roman remains to be found all along the course of Tyne.

Arbeia Fort- South Shields

Chesters Fort - Nr Corbridge

Corbridge Roman Town - Nr Corbridge

Housesteads Fort - Nr Bardon Mill

Segedunum Fort- Wallsend

Vindolanda Fort - Nr Bardon Mill

Roman Names For Local Places

Benwell	Condercum
Corbridge	Corstopitum or Coriosopitum
Newcastle upon Tyne	Pons Aelius or Pons Aelii
South Shields	Arbeia
Tyne	Tinea
Wallsend	Segedunum

Major Castles

* Alnwick - home of the Duke of Northumberland

* Aydon - fortified manor house

* Bamburgh - restored in 19th century

* Chillingham - medieval family fortress

* Dilston - romantic ruin

* Dunstanburgh - ruined 14th century castle

* Etal - 14th century castle

* Lindisfarne - built in 1530

* Newcastle - outstanding views of Tyneside

* Norham - partially distroyed in 1513

* Prudhoe - Norman castle

* Tynemouth - a great view of the harbour

* Warkworth - impressive 12th century castle

Kings & Queens

* King Arthur is reputed to have held court at a castle at Sewingshields Craggs close to Hadrian's Wall.

* King Charles I was held prisoner in Newcastle for ten months during 1646.

* King Edwin's palace, Ad Gefrin was in the Cheviots at Yeavering Bell, Wooler.

* King of the Scots, Malcolm Canmore was killed during a raid on Alnwick and is buried at Tynemouth monastry.

* After Queen Victoria was asked to pay for her meal at a function in Newcastle, she insisted on having the curtains of the Royal train drawn when ever she passed through Newcastle.

* When Queen Victoria decided to stay at Cragside instead of with The Duke of Northumberland, people were shocked that she would turn down the Duke.

Major Battles & Military Events

79	Romans reach the River Tyne
296	Hadrian's Wall is attacked by local tribes revolting against the Romans
343	Risingham and Rochester forts on Hadrian's Wall burnt down
388	Romans on Hadrian's Wall are defeated in battles with local tribes
399	Roman troops start evacuating Britain
410	Nearly all Roman soldiers have left Britain
537	King Arthur of the Britons is believed to have died on Hadrian's Wall fighting Anglo-Saxons
547	King Ida the Flamebearer captures Bamburgh
635	Battle of Heavenfield near Hexham, King Oswald defeats Penda of Mercia
652	Penda, King of Mercia, Ethelwald, King of Deira, attack Northumbria
759	Oswulf, King of Northumbria, murdered at Great Whittington near Corbridge
794	Jarrow monastery attacked by Vikings
800	Tynemouth monastery attacked by Vikings
875	Tynemouth Priory destroyed by Danes
933	Olaf and Swein Forkbeard attack Bamburgh
1067	Copsig appointed Earl of Northumberland then captured and beheaded at Newburn

1157	King Henry reclaims Northumberland from the Scots
1216	King John attacks Northumberland and burns Morpeth, Alnwick and Berwick
1297	William Wallace from Scotland attacks Northumberland; burning Hexham, Corbridge and Ryton
1388	Battle of Otterburn; Scots forces camped at Otterburn are attacked by Harry Hotspur who loses more than 1,000 soldiers whilst the Scots only 200
1402	Battle of Humbleton Hill near Wooler
1462	Alnwick and Bamburgh captured by Lancastrians with the help of the French and Scots, two years later they surrender to King Edward IV
1513	Battle of Flodden Field; James IV of Scotland fought the English led by the Earl of Surrey
1640	Battle of Newburn on Tyne; Scots cross the Tyne and seize Newcastle, a year later the Scots leave after being paid £60,000
1644	Scots capture Newcastle after a ten week siege

Where did the name 'Geordie' come from?

There is no definitive answer. However, according to information provided by the Local Studies Centre at Newcastle City Library there are five possible explanations. There is a fair chance that the term 'Geordie' is derived in some way from the name George, but who knows?

Locally, the term is used to describe people from Tyneside. Throughout Britain and the rest of the world anyone from the North-East is affectionately considered to be a 'Geordie'.

1   During the 1745 Jacobite Rebellion Newcastle was bypassed by the Jacobites, as it was a securely guarded garrison that supported King George. It was said that the region was all "for George" - leading to the name 'Geordie' derived from George.

2   The Oxford English Dictionary states that the word was first used in 1876 to describe miners/pitmen. So perhaps the name originated from the region's coal mines.

3   George Stephenson's miner's lamp was used by local miners in preference to the Davy lamp. The lamp and miners, in time became known as 'Geordies'. The Oxford English Dictionary recognises the first use of the term in an 1881 mining glossary.

4   When George Stephenson addressed a Parliamentary Commission "his blunt speech and dialect drew contemptuous sneers". From then on,colliers (boats taking coal from Tyneside to

London) and the men who worked on them were called 'Geordies'.

5   It is suggested by Frank Graham that 'Geordie' was originally a term of abuse first used by local showman Billy Purvis to put down a rival. This was in 1823, when the word was used in this context due to the unpopularity of King George III who became insane. George IV, his son, was also unpopular due to his extravagance and promiscuity, thereby perpetuating its use.

Historians

Sir Hugh Trevor Roper (Baron Dacre)

From Glanton, Northumberland, he edited Goebbel's diaries and was a highly respected historian. It is perhaps ironic that he is best known for authenticating Hitler's diaries which were later revealed to be a hoax.

Dame Cicely Veronica Wedgewood

A notable English historian from Stocksfield. A 17th century specialist, also known for her biographies of Cromwell and Strafford.

Museums

It is advisable to check opening times in advance of visiting a museum.

Antiquities, Greek Art, Archaeology, University of Newcastle

Roman, Near Eastern, Celtic, Greek artefacts.

Armstrong Household and Farming, Alnwick,

Northumbrian life explored in six rooms.

Berwick Barracks and Borough

Army history in the border town that has apparently had more sieges than Jerusalem.

Berwick Town Hall and Cell Block

History and artefacts of bygone Berwick

Brigantium Archaeological Park, Rochester

A collection of reconstructed Roman and pre-Roman buildings.

Chantry Bagpipe, Morpeth

Northumbrian pipes and pipes from throughout the world.

History

Cherryburn, Mickley, Nr Stocksfield

The birthplace of Thomas Bewick now houses an exhibition celebrating his life and work.

Grace Darling, Bamburgh

The life and times of perhaps the greatest Victorian heroine.

Discovery, Newcastle

Home of the Turbinia, history of Newcastle, science and engineering.

George Stephenson's Birthplace, Wylam

The 17th century cottage where the father of the railways was born.

Hancock, Newcastle

Natural history from dinosaurs to contemporary wildlife.

Heritage Centre, Bellingham.

Exhibitions of railways and everyday life.

House of Hardy, Alnwick

The world's finest fishing tackle manufacturer.

Kirkharle Courtyard, Nr Wallington

A celebration of Capability Brown considered by

many to be Britains greatest landscape gardener. The museum also houses a collection of vintage bicycles.

Military Vehicle, Exhibition Park, Newcastle

Over 50 wartime and post-war vehicles collected by members of the North East Military Vehicle Club.

Old Gaol, Hexham

The museum is located in the first purpose-built gaol (jail) in England - built in 1330 to imprison convicted Reivers. Now houses an exhibition on Reiving.

South Shields Town Museum
Celebrates the history of South Shields its people and history.

Woodhorn Colliery , Ashington

Mining and social history.

Wylam Railway, Wylam

Celebrates local railway pioneers.

Religion

Religious Leaders

Venerable Bede of Jarrow

Bede - ordained in 703, a great scholar, almost all that is currently known about early Anglo-Saxon Britain is from Bede's work.

William Booth

The leader, founder and General of the Salvation Army was converted in 1844 and became a Methodist New Connection minister in Gateshead. The equality of women within the Salvation Army is considered to be due to the influence of his wife Catherine. They lived on Woodbine Terrace, off Coatsworth Road, §before they left the area for London where they set-up the Salvation Army in the East End of London.

St. Chad

He has been incorrectly referred to as the "patron saint of disputed elections", he was born in Northumberland in 620.

Cuthbert

After travelling around Northumbria he spent much of his life as a hermit. Appointed the Prior of

Lindisfarne in 664, then Bishop of Lindisfarne in 685. He resigned the post in 686 and died a year later on Inner Farne Island with only seals and birds for company. Whilst he achieved great fame during his life, his fame has grown tremendously since his death. He is credited as the inspiration behind the Lindisfarne Gospels.

Cardinal Hume

Archbishop of Westminster, Newcastle born Basil Hume is celebrated at Newcastle's Roman Catholic cathedral where his statue can be seen.

Robert Lee

Born in Tweedmouth in 1804 and educated in Berwick where he worked part-time as a boat builder. He went on to become a prominent Scottish theologian and in 1857 started to reform the Presbyterian church service: he restored the reading of prayers, kneeling at prayer, standing during singing. When he introduced a harmonium and then an organ to his church he was bitterly attacked for his innovations.

Joseph Parker

The son of a stonecutter, he was born in Hexham in 1830. He wrote many religious works including *The Peoples' Bible*.

Buildings, Structures & Architecture

Niklaus Pevsner, the distinguished architectural historian, described Newcastle as the best designed Victorian town and large city in England.

Newcastle city centre has more listed classical Georgian buildings than anywhere else in England other than Bath and London.

Grey Street has been voted the best street in Britain by listeners of Radio 4's *Today* programme.

The Byker Wall has attracted international attention not only for its striking design, but also for the thought given when rehousing people from Byker's demolished terraces.

The Sage Centre has been designed by world famous architect Norman Foster.

Architects and Builders

*   ***Ove Arup*** - projects include the Sydney Opera House and Byker Viaduct.

*   ***John Dobson*** - his designs and buildings are all over Newcastle.

*   ***Richard Grainger*** - so influential that the term 'Grainger Town' has been adopted.

*   ***John Green*** - designed the 'Lit and Phil', Theatre Royal and the column for Grey's monument.

Unique Buildings

Tyneside Flats

The characteristic Tyneside flat design dates from the 1840s, the arrangement of upstairs and downstairs flats being rarely seen outside the region.

The ground floor has a long entrance corridor that leads to a large front bedroom, smaller back bedroom and living room. The kitchen is located behind the living room. Originally the back door would lead to the yard, toilet and coal house. Recently bathrooms have been added to the kitchen end.

The upstairs is the same as downstairs, except for the addition of a small bedroom above the downstairs entrance corridor.

Legislation was passed in 1892 stipulating that the minimum distance between terraces should be 40 ft at the front and 20 ft at the rear.

The frontage had to have a minimum width of 18 ft and the minimum size for an inhabitable room has been set at 70 sq ft.

Pele Towers

Built as a safeguard against marauding Scots, a number date from as early as the 13th century, Pele Towers continued to be built until about 1600. As one would expect from a defensive building, they were constructed from large, heavy stone. The ground floor was vaulted and used to store food and livestock. A spiral staircase built into one corner led upstairs to one, two, or three storeys.

Only the more affluent would have been able to live in a Pele Tower.

Bastle Houses

Fortified houses built mainly from the mid-16th century until the mid-17th century to protect the family against 'reivers'. Rectangular in plan with external dimensions of 35 ft x 25 ft with two storeys of steeply pitched gables. At their base the stone walls would be about 4 ft thick, thinning out to 3½ ft at the first floor. Access to the upper floor was through an external staircase or possibly a wooden ladder. Livestock would be kept secure on the ground floor and the family would shelter above.

Staithes

Designed to speed up the loading of coal from land to waiting colliers by means of a chute or spout. As early as 1771 Keelman staged strikes and protested against the building of staithes by the river mouth. It was not until 1820 that the first direct-loading coal staithes gained a foothold on the lower reaches of the Tyne.

Dunston Staithes is the best example remaining, (unfortunately damaged by a recent fire) and is a scheduled Ancient Monument. The first stage was completed in 1893 and a second stage was opened in 1903. It stretched over 550 yards and had three loading berths; each with two spouts at different levels to enable loading whatever the level of the tide. On completion it was believed to be the largest wooden structure in the world. It remained in use until 1983 and at its peak, in the 1920s, it handled 140,000 tons of coal a week.

Old Tyne Bridges

Roman

The first recorded bridge across the Tyne was Roman. Built by Emperor Hadrian circa 122. It was destroyed by fire in 1248.

Built on the site of the current swing-bridge, the crossing was named Pons Aelius in honour of the family name. The family crest depicting a goat's head was apparently fixed to the southern end of the bridge. It is therefore possible that the name Gateshead is a corruption of 'goat'shead'.

Medieval

Built using the remains of the Roman bridge circa 1250. It was virtually destroyed by the Great Flood of 1771 with the loss of six lives.

Georgian

Built on the alignment of the Roman and Medieval bridges, officially opened in 1781, it was aesthetically pleasing but flawed. Its broad piers and abutments occupied a third of the total waterway. In effect the bridge acted as a weir, making navigation difficult at times and dredging impractical.

Notable Current Tyne Bridges

Gateshead Millennium Bridge

The unique tilting design is a world first for Tyneside and is now a famous landmark. Operating like a giant eyelid, turning on pivots on both sides of the river, the 600 metric tonne structure has a headroom of 50 m. The bridge provides a pedestrian and cycle link between Newcastle and Gateshead quayside.

The 2002 'Building of the Year' from the Royal Fine Art Commission Trust and British Sky Broadcasting, it is the first bridge to win the award.

Swingbridge

Commissioned following the problems with the Georgian Bridge, William Armstrong designed, engineered and built the bridge which opened in 1876 and still works. Over 500,000 ships have passed by.

When it opened it was the largest bridge of its type in the world.

It is possible to have a guided tour of the mechanical systems that operate the bridge during the annual heritage weekend.

Tyne Bridge

For many years the Tyne Bridge has been the symbol of Tyneside. Construction began in 1925 and it was opened in 1928 by King George V. Often compared to the Sydney Harbour Bridge which was started before the Tyne Bridge, but did not open until 1932.

The towers have little structural value and apparently were designed as five storey warehouses but the floors were never installed. Lifts were incorporated to allow access to the quayside for goods and passengers.

When it opened it was the largest single span bridge in Britain.

High Level Bridge

Designed and built by Robert Stephenson and T.E. Harrison, trains use the upper level, road vehicles use the lower level.

When opened by Queen Victoria in 1849 a Mr Williamson jumped from the parapet into the river for a bet to win a quart of beer. He survived to claim his prize.

King Edward VII Bridge

The phenomenal growth of rail travel led to the construction of a second railway bridge, opened by King Edward VII in 1906.

Queen Elizabeth II Metro Bridge

The Metro was designed to be part of Britain's first fully-integrated transport system, which Mrs Thatcher's government later rejected.

Opened by Queen Elizabeth II in 1981.

Redheugh Bridge (new)

The current Redheugh bridge is the third and was opened by the Princess of Wales in 1983.

It is rumoured that when engineers carried out routine structural checks on the previous (second) bridge, they checked the bridge at both banks but used an alternative bridge crossing.

Newburn Bridge

The present iron bridge was built in 1854 and replaced a ferry that operated from the Boathouse Inn. It was the last bridge to charge a toll.

Wylam Road Bridge

Built in 1835, the superstructure was renewed and widened in 1960. The original toll-house can still be seen on the north-west corner of the bridge.

Wylam Old Bridge

The first single arch bridge built for a railway crossing. Building started in 1874, it closed to traffic and is now popular with walkers and cyclists. It looks like a baby Tyne Bridge.

Corbridge

A solid and beautiful seven arch bridge dating from 1674, the single lane is controlled by traffic lights.

Hexham

The first bridge was built in 1770 and was washed away in floods a year later. The 1780 replacement lasted only two years, the third and current dates from 1793.

Notable North Tyne Bridges

Chollerford Bridge

A five arch bridge built in 1775 following the destruction of an earlier bridge in the Great Flood of 1771.

Bellingham Bridge

Until the bridge was built in 1834 it was necessary to cross the river by a dangerous ford that had claimed many lives over the years.

Kielder Viaduct

Originally built for the North Tyne Valley railway, now preserved and listed.

Notable South Tyne Bridges

Haydon Bridge

The old bridge built in 1774 is now scheduled as an Ancient Monument and pedestrianised.

Ridley Bridge

Built in 1792, to link Ridley Hall with the main east-west highway, by J. Mylne who also built the Georgian Tyne Bridge.

Haltwhistle Bridge

The 'Blue Bridge' was opened in 1851 as a railway viaduct for the now extinct Alston branch line. Now used by pedestrians and cyclists.

Featherstone Bridge

It has an unusual lopsided appearance because the keystone and the peak of the arch are out of alignment.

Lambley Viaduct

A magnificent viaduct designed by Sir George Barclay Bruce, now part of the South Tyne Trail.

Eals Bridge

Built in 1733 and designed to avoid flood damage. As it is still here clearly the design works.

Tyne Tunnels

Tyne Pedestrian & Cycle Tunnel

When completed in 1951, the approach escalators with an 85 ft vertical fall were the longest continuous escalators in the world and the first to permit use by cyclists.

Tyne Road Tunnel

Opened in 1967 it is 5,400 ft in length and reaches a maximum depth of 80 ft.

Politicians, Campaigners & Philosophers

George Fife Angus

A Newcastle ship owner, he founded South Australia; appointed commissioner for the formation of the colony in 1834.

Lord William Beveridge

The architect of the Welfare State was M.P. for Berwick. In 1942 he wrote the *Report on Social Insurance and Allied Services*.

He is buried in Throckington churchyard in Northumberland.

Thomas Burt

Born in South Shields in 1837, he was the first working miner to become an M.P. (Morpeth) and in time became the Father of the House of Commons.

William Fox

Born in South Shields in 1812. He left the region for New Zealand. Elected Prime Minister on four occasions.

James Redpath

An American reformer and journalist, he was born in Berwick in 1833 and his family emigrated in 1850. He publicised the actions of the 'American Labor Movement'.

Nicholas Ridley

Born in Newcastle in 1929, he held three cabinet posts and was considered to be one of Margaret Thatcher's closest allies.

Thomas Spence

A leading 18th century philosopher and socialist. His father was from Aberdeen and a member of a religious sect called the Glassites which believed in the idea of a community of goods. Thomas Spence was one of the first people to lecture to the then recently formed Philosophical Society in Newcastle (it preceded the Lit. and Phil.) where he spoke on his plan for common land ownership. When he was gathering wild nuts in a wood he was confronted and accused of stealing. He pointed out that squirrels and wild animals were able to gather and eat nuts. If he was not allowed to enjoy 'gifts of nature' his status as a human was less than that of a wild animal.

William Thomas Stead

An English reformer and journalist, born at Embleton. After editing the *Northern Echo* he took the same job at the *Pall Mall*. He raised public awareness of the practice of purchasing child prostitutes by committing the offence himself and writing a feature article about it. He was imprisoned for three months, but his campaigning led to a change in the law.

Radical Women

Mary Astell (1666 - 1731)

A pioneering feminist born in the quayside area of Newcastle, who is considered to be the first published feminist. *A Serious Proposal To The Ladies* was published in 1694 and *Some Reflections Upon Marriage* followed in 1700.

Josephine Butler (1828 - 1906)

Born in Milfield, her family moved to Dilston when she was seven. She worked with destitute women and prostitutes in Liverpool in 1866, pressing for educational and employment opportunities for women. She successfully campaigned for the repeal of the Contagious Diseases Act.

Sarah Emily Davies (1830 - 1921)

Set up the Society for the Employment of Women in Gateshead and was a leading suffragette. She campaigned for female education and founded Girton College, Cambridge.

Emily Wilding Davison (1872 - 1913)

From Longhorsley, near Morpeth; Emily was a highly active suffragette and was imprisoned several times where she was force-fed. When she barricaded herself into her cell the prison authorities tried to drown her with a hose-pipe, she later became ill. She died when she jumped in front of the King's horse at the Derby on June 4th 1913.

Margaret Grace Bondfield (1873-1953)

The Labour M.P. for Wallsend was the first female cabinet member (1929-31). She had also been the first female chair of the T.U.C. in 1923.

Anna Howard Shaw (1847 - 1919)

Born in Newcastle, she moved to the States when she was four. For a number of years, from 1888, she worked with women's rights leader Susan B Anthony. Anna was president of the National American Suffrage Association from 1904-1915.

Ellen Wilkinson M.P. (1891 - 1947)

Became M.P. for Jarrow in 1935 and supported the Jarrow Hunger March in 1936. Nicknamed 'Red Ellen', she recently and posthumously received the honour of having a beer named after her (see Jarrow Brewery).

Unknown

Suffragettes burnt down Gosforth Hall at Gosforth Racecourse. The local constabulary failed to find those responsible (any information please ring Crimestoppers on 0800 555 111).

Law & Order

*   When Robert de Pykewell was the vicar of Haltwhistle, he had the misfortune of being kidnapped by Scottish raiders who demanded a ransom. The good people of Haltwhistle decided that the Scots could keep their vicar.

*   The 'Newcastle Witch Trial' of 1649 found 27 out of 30 witches guilty; 14 were executed on the Town Moor.

*   In the Hexham riots of 1761 it is believed that about 50 protesters were killed and hundreds injured when soldiers opened fire on them. It was one of a series of protests against the introduction of balloting to select men for three years military service.

*   In 1763, to maintain law and order in Newcastle, people were employed to patrol the streets equipped with a rattle and a hook on a stick. It is thought that they worked only at night.

*   A postman from South Shields was executed on the Town Moor in Newcastle in 1776 for stealing a letter with two £50 notes attached from Newcastle Post Office.

*   Alnmouth was attacked by pirate Paul Jones from his ship The Ranger, in 1779.

*   In August 1832 William Jobling was the last man to be publicly gibbeted at Jarrow Slake.

*   The Chief Constable of Newcastle's 1836 report identified 71 brothels and 46 houses of ill repute. 18 years later in 1854 more than a 100 brothels and 500 public houses and beer shops were identified.

*   The world's first use of a car in a 'police chase' took place in Newcastle in 1900. A policeman commandeered a car and its driver to pursue a drunk on a horse. A mile later the drunk was successfully apprehended.

*   In recent history riots have taken place in Elswick in the west end of Newcastle and the Meadowell Estate, North Shields.

Scientists

Thomas Addison

Born in Longbenton, he founded endocrinology and was the first person to describe the symptoms of adrenal insufficiency which is now known as Addison's disease.

It was his work at Guy's Hospital that established the institution as a famous medical school.

Sir George Airy

From Alnwick, a geophysicist and astronomer with an impressive list of achievements in a long scientific career.

He determined the mass of the earth from gravitational measurements in mines (mines in South Shields were used for early scientific experiments in gravity due to their depth). Airy invented a cylindrical lens for the correction of astigmatism. He promoted Greenwich Mean Time (measured using Airy's telescope with his observatory on the line of zero longitude), it became Britain's legal time in 1880 when Airy started the practice of sending out time signals by telegraph.

He is sometimes incorrectly credited with discovering Neptune. Airy was, however Astronomer Royal when the planet was discovered.

Neil Bartlett

Neil Bartlett was born in Newcastle. Inert gases were believed to be elements that were unable to form molecules with other elements, he discovered that they could combine with selected other elements and were therefore not absolutely inert.

Arthur Holmes

From Hebburn on Tyne, Arthur developed the dating of rocks and the measurement of radioactive decay in uranium. One of his major achievements was the dating of the earth.

Harold Jeffreys

Studied at Armstrong College in Newcastle and became a reader in geophysics at Cambridge. He was the first person to put forward the view that the earth's centre is molten lava.

Alison Murdoch

Based at the Fertility Centre at Newcastle University, she is one of only two people in Britain legally allowed to clone human embryos.

Sir George Pickering

From Whalton in Northumberland, a pioneer in the study of blood pressure. He regularly appeared on the radio and was one of the first media-friendly 'popular scientists'.

Lewis Fry Richardson

A mathematician who was the first to apply mathematics to weather prediction, a method that he termed 'weather prediction by finite differences'.

Matt Ridley

Chairman of the International Centre for Life, Matt Ridley is a leading writer of popular science books and a leading authority on the human genome, which investigates the link between genes and the individual.

Stanley Keith Runcorn

He Worked at Newcastle University where he studied the ancient magnetic patterns in British rocks.

John Snow

He studied at Newcastle Medical School (founded in 1832), and controversially used chloroform on Queen Victoria. He was a leading developer of public health policy, in particular in relation to cholera and the water supply in London.

William Turner

The 'Father of English Botany' was born in Morpeth. His *Herbal*, published in three parts, was the first in English containing original material. He identified and named numerous plant species.

Inventors

*Gladstone Adams - **Windscreen Wiper***

A photographer from Whitley Bay, he patented an early windscreen wiper in 1911. A model of his design can be seen at the Discovery Museum in Newcastle. His brother apparently invented the sliding seat used in rowing boats.

*William George Armstrong - **Hydraulic Crane***

Born in Newcastle. With the riches from his armaments factory he bought and refurbished Bamburgh Castle. He also built Cragside (which was the first house lit by hydroelectricity) and a large stately house in Jesmond Dene. William Armstrong invented the hydraulic crane and an innovative side-loading battle gun.

*Hunter Carr - **Whale Perfume***

From Jarrow, he invented a way to make perfume from whale oil. Quite rightly this is not considered environmentaly friendly and would now be illegal.

*Bryan Donkin - **Paper Making Machine***

From Sandhoe, Northumberland. Bryan Donkin developed the first automatic paper making machine, nearly 200 of which were manufactured. He also invented and patented a rotary printing press, but this was not a success. Bryan Donkin improved on Frenchman Appert methods of food processing and built a factory to supply the Royal Navy with canned meat and vegetables.

John James Fenwick - **Trilby Hat**

After opening his first department store at 5 Northumberland Street in 1882, he opened a shop in London in 1891. A few years later there was a London stage production of George Du Maurier's 'Trilby', with leading lady Dorothea Baird who had been born on the site of his Newcastle shop. John James Fenwick made her a gown, costume and soft felt hat complete with narrow brim and indented crown. This was the first trilby hat.

Arthur George - **Control Column (Joy Stick)**

A Newcastle motor engineer who built aircraft as a hobby, Arthur George wanted to overcome the problem of having to use several levers to control each part of an aircraft. He designed a multi-pivoted 'control column' from spare motor parts and patented his invention in 1909.

The term 'joystick' was coined by early aviators who flew in the First World War. They had difficult cramped conditions so clearly considered it a 'joy' to be able to control many of the aeroplane's functions with one column, conveniently placed between their legs.

Forster Hardy - **Fishing Reel**

The 'Perfect Fishing Reel' was patented by Forster Hardy in 1888. His design used ball bearings so that the reel was "smooth and fast running", enabling fishermen to cast further. The company that he founded is still making fishing tackle; Alnwick based, House of Hardy has a world wide reputation manufacturing the highest quality fishing rods and reels.

William Hogget - **Flavoured Crisps**

The first ever flavoured crisps are believed to have been invented by William Hogget of Whickham, Gateshead, who developed vinegar flavour crisps.

John Henry Holmes - **Light Switch**

Inventor of the electric light switch in 1884, it was then called the 'quick break' switch as it had the familiar snap off action that is still in use today.

William Horner - **The Lift**

William Horner patented a design for a lift mechanism in 1818 and installed it in the Coliseum building in Regents Park in 1829. The lift, and Horner's designs did not take off. It was not until 1861, when Otis patented the safety lift that lifts became trusted.

John Morrison - **Transparent Sticking Plaster**

John Morrison invented transparent adhesive sticking plaster; he also manufactured, marketed and sold his invention. Chemists sold his plasters in penny packets which were supplied by the gross, carriage free, for seven shillings.

W.R. Pape - *Breach-Loading Firearms*

A gunsmith with premises at the junction of Westgate Road and Collingwood Street in Newcastle, he is attributed with the invention of the breach-loading firearm.

Charles Parsons - *Steam Turbine*

Whilst working for Clarke, Chapman and Co. in Gateshead he developed the steam turbine (1884). He went on to design and make Turbinia, the world's first steam turbine ship and at the time (1887) it was the world's fastest ship. Turbinia can be seen at the Discovery Museum in Newcastle. His turbines were used in the Lusitania and the Mauritania.

Parsons' other innovations include: more efficient screw propellers, searchlights and optical systems. He is one of Tyneside's greatest Victorian engineers, industrialists and entrepreneurs.

Joseph Wilson Swan - *Light Bulb*

Swan invented the incandescent light bulb which he demonstrated at the 'Lit. and Phil.' in Newcastle. A manufacturing plant was set up in Benwell.

Swan was also responsible for the development of the dry photographic process which enabled photography to be enjoyed by 'the masses' as it was no longer necessary to have a laboratory to take and process photographs. The photographic technology developed by Swan is the principle behind photographic film. He also invented a system of duplication (bromide photography) which has been universally used until recently being replaced by digital technology.

William Boutland Wilkinson - **Reinforced Concrete**

Newcastle based William Wilkinson invented reinforced concrete and was known to be using the technique as early as 1854. He did not take out a patent for his invention which 'paved' the way for Frenchman Joseph Monier to do so in 1867.

John Woodger - **Kippers**

Kippers are believed to have been invented by John Woodger, in Seahouses, by accident in 1843. He left herring on a rack overnight over a burning fire. At first he thought that the fish would have been ruined, he discovered that the fish were wonderful!

William Woodhave - **Self-Righting Lifeboat**

As with many inventions, there is dispute about who invented the first self-righting lifeboat. After the 'Adventure of Newcastle' sank losing all on board, a committee was formed and the decision was taken to run a competition to design and build a lifeboat. William Woodhave's designs were incorporated into a model that was submitted by Henry Greathead and accepted by the competition committee. Who designed the first lifeboat, Greathead or Woodhave?

Industry

Coal

Coal was a significant driving force in the industrial development of Tyneside and Northumberland.

The need to transport coal led to the region becoming the birthplace of the railway and a world-class ship making centre. The demand for ropes for use in mines led to a number of rope factories, particularly on Gateshead quayside. Skills from the rope making industry were transferred into cable making. The world's first transatlantic telegraph cable was made in Gateshead.

Shipping coal to London made many mine owners phenomenally wealthy. It is believed that the first shipment of coal to London was in 1305 on the 'Welfare'.

At one time the term 'Wallsend Coal' was the generic term given to the premium grade of house coal. Customers who wished to order the highest grade coal continued requesting 'Wallsend Coal' long after it ceased to be mined in Wallsend.

Buckingham Palace used to source coal from Shilbottle Colliery, near Alnwick. It was the Royal Family's coal of choice because it produced low quantities of ash.

Coal attracted glass makers from all over the country and indeed from the Continent.

Glass

Jarrow was the first place in England to manufacture stained glass.

The Delavals developed the Royal Northumberland Bottle Works at Seaton Sluice. In 1762 this was the country's largest glass works.

Towards the end of the 17th century the Italian Dagnia glass making family arrived in Newcastle from Bristol. It is probable that they introduced lead glass and quality glass making to the area, whilst previously only sheet glass and bottles had been made.

The renowned and internationally famous *Newcastle Style* of balusters (glass goblets) are highly collectable: tall, with multi-knopped stems often with rows of tiny air beads and clear white metal. Key figures in the development of the style were William and Mary Beilby. In the 1760s they developed techniques using coloured and white enamels to decorate glassware. Their elaborate decorative stems had delicate twists and were much copied by other glass makers, particularly in the Netherlands but also other countries on the Continent.

Fishing

The fishing industry for many generations employed thousands of people in Tyneside and Northumberland. Prior to the First World War North Shields was considered to be the premier white fish port in Britain.

During the Second World War it was not safe to fish in the North Sea; but immediately following the war record catches were made for a few years. Sadly, the fishing industry is rapidly becoming a distant memory; fish numbers have declined, fish are significantly smaller, they are maturing younger, and the future is bleak.

Transport

Railway

The North-East gave the world the railway. The very first railways were horse-drawn and used for transporting coal.

The standard gauge which is used throughout 60% of the world is credited to George Stephenson. One story is that he took an average of cart axle widths when deciding on the guage of 4 ft $8^1/_2$ inches. It has been noted that there is evidence on Hadrian's Wall that the same gauge was used for carts by the Romans; it is also the average width of two horses' backsides.

Early Railway Pioneers

William Brunton

His 'claim to fame' is the design of a locomotive which propelled itself by two steam powered mechanical legs. Much to everyone's surprise it actually worked, but it would only run in one direction which obviously would cause problems. This conundrum was solved when the engine blew up.

William Chapman

In 1812 he built an engine which dragged itself along on a chain. However, the engine could hardly move itself, never mind carry a load. It was soon abandoned.

Daniel Gooch

The first locomotive engineer of the Great Western Railway was born in Bedlington in 1816. He was appointed by I.K. Brunel who needed Daniel Gooch to sort out the problems with his engineering designs. He also laid the first trans-Atlantic telegraph cable.

William Hedley

The manager of Wylam Colliery, he experimented with steam engines and built 'Puffing Billy' in 1813 which ran until 1862. He also built the 'Wylam Dilly'. Both engines used to run on the Wylam Waggonway, past the cottage where George Stephenson was born.

George Stephenson

Considered by many to be the most important figure in the creation of railways.

He worked as a fireman in a colliery and paid to have a rudimentary education at night school. After inventing a safety lamp for use in mines (contemporaneously with Davy), he won a public testimonial of £1,000. His first locomotive was 'Blucher' in 1814. Stephenson was appointed engineer for the construction of the Stockton and Darlington railway which became the first passenger railway. In 1829 at the Rainhill trial he successfully demonstrated his most famous engine 'The Rocket'; Stephenson went on to work as an engineer on railways throughout the country and advise on the construction of railways across the world.

Robert Stephenson

Son of George, born in Willington Quay in 1803, Robert was sent to Edinburgh University for six months. He worked with his father on the Stockton and Darlington railway and became the manager of his father's engine works in Newcastle. His most visible legacy is the High Level Bridge over the Tyne and the Royal Border Bridge in Berwick. He died in 1859 and is buried in Westminster Abbey.

Notable Railway Achievements

Bowes Railway

It is the only surviving rope-worked standard gauge railway. Bowes Railway is to the south of Gateshead and can be visited.

Brandling Junction Railway

Built in 1839, it ran from a connection with the Newcastle-Carlisle railway at Gateshead to Monkwearmouth, Sunderland and South Shields. Much of the route is used today by the Metro. Opposite Felling Metro station is a small stone building beside the B.R. line; this is the original Felling station and is possibly the oldest surviving unaltered railway station in the world.

Newcastle-Carlisle Railway

The Newcastle-Carlisle line was the first coast-to-coast railway.

When it opened on the 18th June 1838 five trains left Carlisle at six in the morning. The first train arrived in Newcastle with the Mayor and Corporation of Carlisle and was conveyed across the river by the Mayor of Newcastle's barge to a reception at the Newcastle Assembly Rooms. When the second train arrived the rush of passengers up the gangway to the ferry caused it to collapse and 12 people had an early bath in the Tyne. 3,500 passengers left on 13 trains for a return trip to Carlisle. The carriages on the trains were mainly open goods wagons with planks fitted for seats. Unfortunately, there were two collisions on the return journey and a thunderstorm. The passengers finally arrived back in Newcastle at six the next day. It must have been an unforgettable trip!

The North Tyneside Loop Line

Still largely used by the Metro, it was electrified in 1904. After the successful launch of the loop line it was decided to open a branch line from Monkseaton to Seaton Sluice, the name Seaton Sluice was considered to be undesirable so Collywell Bay was chosen instead. The First World War broke out, two years after building started, so the rail link was never completed.

Tanfield Railway

Built in 1725 to carry coal to Dunston, the line includes the famous Causey Arch which is the oldest railway bridge in the world. The line finally closed in 1964, part of it is now preserved with a large collection of Tyneside built locomotives. Many rail enthusiasts consider the Tanfield Railway to be the oldest railway still in operation in the world.

Tynemouth Stations

Between 1847 and 1882 the then small town of Tynemouth had no fewer than five different stations. Three were open together from 1864 to 1882 when they were all replaced by the present station.

Boats and Ships

Traditional Boats

Coble

The only surviving indigenous craft of the North-East coast, designed to be launched off open beaches, they still exist at Newbiggin and Boulmer. A coble is built by bending steamed planks to shape with lightweight frames. The method of construction has many similarities to that of Viking longships. The earliest description of a coble dates back to the 16th century, and there was no basic change in design until the 20th century when motors were added. There are fewer than two hundred left and the number regularly fishing is barely in double figures. They are between 25 ft and 35 ft long with a beam of 7 ft to 9 ft.

Keel Boat

A traditionally designed fishing vessel, measuring up to 50 ft long, they sailed from harbours and rivers all along the coast. The disappeared about a hundred years ago, when they were made redundant by modern boats. A few Keel boats can be seen cut in half, upturned and used as huts on Holy Island.

Tyne Keel

A barge used by Keelman to transport coal to colliers at the harbour. They had a key role in the development of the mining industry. Keelmen used to race along the Tyne competing for work.

Notable Ships & Shipbuilding Achievements

* H.M.S. Argo launched at Howden in 1781 was the largest ship built on the Tyne up to that time (with 44 guns).

* S.S. Elbruz an oil tanker, was the first twin screwed diesel engined vessel in the world in 1914, built by the Tyne Iron Shipbuilding Co.

* The John Bowes built in Jarrow in 1852, was the first iron-built steam collier.

* The Dominion Monarch launched on the Tyne in 1838 was at the time the largest motor driven passenger ship in the world.

* Jubilee floating dock left the Tyne for New Zealand in 1931. It is possibly the longest tow on record (14,000 nautical miles).

* The Mauritania was built in 1906 by Swan Hunter, It held the Blue Ribband award for the fastest crossing of the Atlantic for 22 years. Towards the end of its life it became the first cruise ship in the Mediterranean.

* San Fraterno launched in 1913 was the largest tanker in the world, built by Swan Hunter it could carry 15,700 tons of oil.

* Tyne built Sviatogor later renamed the Krasin, became the most famous ship of 1928 after rescuing Nobile's arctic airship expedition. The event was made into a film (The Red Tent) with Peter Finch and Sean Connery.

* The original Arc Royal was built in Blyth.

* The world's first oil tanker, the Gluckhauf was launched by Tyneside shipbuilders Armstrong, Mitchell and Co. in 1886.

* The first supertanker to be built on the Tyne was the Esso Northumbria.

* The largest vessel to sail up the Tyne was the Bonga oil exploration ship in 2002. It weighs 300,000 tonnes which is equivelent to 30,000 double decker buses.

Commerce

Brands

Be-Ro Flour

Self-raising flour was invented by Thomas Bell of Longhorsley. The name is derived from BE(ll) and RO(yal).

Domestos

The number one bleach brand was invented in Newcastle by Wilfred and Ivy Handley in 1929. The former Domestos works in the Ouseburn Valley, Newcastle, is now an art and crafts studio (Test House 5).

They also pioneered the use of soft plastic bottles that could be squeezed for washing-up liquid.

Earl Grey Tea

Now the world's most popular blend of tea.

It was sent as a gift to Prime Minister Earl Grey, after an envoy on a diplomatic mission saved the life of a Chinese Mandarin. Oil of bergamot gives the tea its unique flavour. Earl Grey loved the aroma and flavour so much, he requested his tea merchant, Tyneside company Twinings, to reproduce the blend.

Lucozade

Invented by a Newcastle pharmacist in the 1920s to build up the blood sugar level of children.

Fairy Soap

Originally a Thomas Hedley & Co. product. The company was bought by Proctor and Gamble in the 1930s.

Greggs

Originally a family bakery business founded by John Gregg on Tyneside in 1930. The company now has over 1,200 Greggs and Bakers Oven stores.

Maling Pottery

Founded in Sunderland in 1762, the company moved to Newcastle in 1817 and became the biggest pottery in the world. Now highly collectable, Cetem Ware was launched in 1908 and Maling Ware in the 1920s. Production ceased in 1963. The site is now Hoults Estate (formerly Hoults Removals) and home to a diverse range of businesses.

Newcastle Brown Ale

The recipe for the beer that once could only be brewed in Newcastle was developed by Colonel James Herbert Porter in 1927. It is now the UK's biggest selling premium bottled beer and is brewed in Gateshead at the Federation Brewery.

Tyne Brand

The famous canned food company started producing canned fish but is best known for canned meat products.

Business

Armstrong-Vickers

The company is now part of the Alvis group, based on Scotswood Road. The company has been making tanks and armaments for generations and its roots can be traced back to William Armstrong's famous Elswick Works.

Bainbridge

It is believed to be the oldest department store in the world. The exact date it opened is not known, but is believed to be been during 1838.

Barbour

Manufacturer of the finest waxed coats and outdoor wear. Based in South Shields, they export all over the world.

Barratts

Founded by Sir Lawrence Barratt in 1958, his name is now synonymous with modern housing estates.

Commerce

Greggs

Originally a family bakery business founded by John Gregg on Tyneside in 1930. The company now has over 1,200 Greggs and Bakers Oven stores.

Sage

A FTSE 100 company, born and based in Newcastle, it has grown to become the leading supplier of accountancy software for small to medium sized enterprises.

Ringtons

Set up in 1907 by Sam Smith who moved from Leeds to Newcastle to establish the business with William Titterington. Well known for their home delivery service, they now supply tea to major customers including Marks and Spencer.

Street Markets

Many markets have been established for hundreds of years, some were established by Royal Charter.

Town	_Market Day_
Alnwick	Saturday, Thursday (from Easter)
Amble	Sunday
Ashington	Tuesday
Bedlington	Thursday
Bellingham	Monday
Berwick upon Tweed	Wednesday
Blyth	Friday, Saturday
Cramlington	Wednesday
Haltwhistle	Thursday
Hexham	Tuesday
Morpeth	Wednesday
Newcastle Quayside	Sunday
Rothbury	Friday
Seahouses	Friday (summer only)
South Shields	Monday, Saturday,Wednesday (April-December)

Specialist Markets

Over the last few years there has been a growth in niche or specialist markets. The explosion in farmers markets has enabled consumers to buy traditionally produced food regularly.

Craft, Art & Collectable	*Market Day*
Jesmond Dene (Arts/Crafts) Armstrong Bridge	Sunday
South Shields (Flea) Market Square	Saturday
Tynemouth (Flea) Metro Station	Saturday, Sunday

A livestock market held outside of Morpeth used to be the biggest in the UK behind Smithfield.

The Bigg Market, Newcastle, takes its name from a type of barley called 'bigg' that farmers used to sell in an area that has now become a legendary destination for revellers.

When the Grainger Market opened in Newcastle in 1835 it was the largest and finest in Britain. Two acres in area with 14 entrances, 243 shops and two massive ornamental fountains where ducks brought for sale on market day were allowed to swim.

Farmers Markets

Town & Location	_Day of The Month_
Alnwick	last Friday
Market Place	
Blyth	first Saturday
Market Place Cobbles	
Hexham	second Saturday
Agricultural Auction Mart	
Morpeth	first Sunday
Town Hall	
Newcastle	first Friday
Grainger Street	
Ponteland	fourth Saturday
County High School	
South Shields	every Wednesday
Market Square	
Tynemouth	third Saturday
Metro Station	

Early Closing Days

Traditionally towns used to have an early closing day. Most shops in the towns listed below will be open at least six days a week, but a few shops continue the practice of early closing one day a week.

Town	_Day_
Alnwick	Wednesday
Amble	Wednesday
Berwick upon Tweed	Thursday
Hexham	Wednesday
Morpeth	Thursday
Seahouses	Wednesday
Tynemouth	Wednesday

Art

Artists

For an authoritative reference on the region's artists the best source of information is the work of Marshall Hall.

Thomas Bewick

Born at Cherryburn, near Mickley, he spent most of his working life in Newcastle. Arguably the region's most influential artist and a world renowned wood-engraver. He is best known for his wildlife engravings, and also worked on children's books.

John Wilson Carmichael

Famous for seascapes, some of which can be seen in the Laing Gallery, Newcastle.

Ronald Embleton

A Londoner, he met Tyneside publisher Frank Graham when on holiday in Tunisia. He produced over 140 paintings featuring the North-East. Over six million postcards have been sold of his scenes of Roman life; the best selling postcard featuring Roman soldiers on the latrine has sold over a million! His main body of work was comic strips and boys own annuals.

Jimmy Forsyth

His photographs of the people of Scotswood and Tyneside have received both critical and popular acclaim. A number of books are available featuring his work.

Gilroy

From Whitley Bay, famous for his advertising artwork produced for Guinness which made dubious but amusing claims such as *"Guinness Is Good For You"*. When he was 15 he drew sketches of theatrical entertainers for the Evening Chronicle.

Ralph Hedley

A member of the famous 'Cullercoats' school of artists. One of his most popular works is of a painting of a cat which has been displayed at the Laing Gallery Newcastle with the title 'Cat In The Cottage Window'. Recently the title 'Blinking In The Sunlight' was found written on the reverse of the painting. Whatever the name, the painting has been loved by children and adults for generations.

John Martin

From Haydon Bridge, he attended the famous Shaftoe Trust Grammar school which provided free education for children. He went on to become an internationally recognised artist, achieving fame for his oil paintings of biblical scenes. It is thought that he probably used local scenes as a backdrop.

Thomas Miles Richardson

The leading Newcastle artist of the first half of the 19th century and the first Tyneside artist to produce large oil paintings. He organised the first art exhibition in Newcastle in 1822 and established the first purpose-built art gallery in 1827.

Ron Thornton

Born in South Shields, he has lived for many years in Riding Mill. Ron has painted all his life and decided to retire early from a career in education to paint professionally. A collection of his watercolours and sketches *The River Tyne From Sea to Source* has become a best seller.

Ten Monuments

There are hundreds of sculptures and monuments many of which are historic and serve as a permanent reminder of past achievements, heroes and heroines. Recently there has been a renaissance in public art.

The Angel of the North, *Gateshead*

Designed by Antony Gormley, in just a few years this symbol of the gateway to Tyneside has become a national icon. It is seen by 90,000 people every day.

Admiral Collingwood, *Pier Road, Tynemouth*

Collingwood took control of the navy when Nelson was killed. On Trafalgar Day throughout the Royal Navy a tune is whistled and verse is read for Nelson, apart from at the Royal Navy base on Gateshead quayside where Collingwood is celebrated.

Joseph Cowan, *Westgate Road/Fenkle Street*

Social reformer, M.P for Newcastle 1873 - 1886 (his father had also been M.P. for Newcastle), he bought the Evening Chronicle in 1862 and founded the Tyne Theatre and Opera House.

Grace Darling, *Bamburgh*

Grace Darling lived with her father on the Longstone Lighthouse. She rescued nine sailors from the steamship Forfarshire sailing from Hull to Dundee, in a storm on September 7th 1838.

Earl Grey, *Newcastle*

The sculpture is by Edward Hughes Bailey, who was also responsible for Nelson on Nelson's Column. The statue was struck by lightning in 1942 and his head fell off. It was replaced in 1947. Earl Grey not only has a blend of tea named after him, he is also one of the greatest parliamentarians ever. He succeeded in getting the Reform Bill through the House of Commons (it took three attempts). It enabled the reformed parliament to abolish slavery in the colonies.

It is possible to climb the column, however it is only open a few days every year.

Hartley Colliery Disaster, *Earsdon*

Many miners have lost their lives in mining accidents. This monument commemorates one of the worst.

204 men and boys died in the Hartley disaster in January 1862. It brought forward legislation that required all mines to have two alternative means of access/exit i.e two shafts.

Stan Laurel, *Dockwray Square, North Shields*

Stan Laurel lived some of his early life in North Shields. It is believed that the inspiration behind the Laurel and Hardy film, where they move a piano up a flight of stairs was gained after Stan watched a North Shields family move their household belongings up the steps from the fish quay.

Jackie Milburn, St James Boulevard

Arguably Newcastle United's greatest player, the statue was built by public subscription (*Evening Chronicle* readers). It was originally sited on Northumberland Street.

Tenantry Column, Alnwick

Built in 1815 with a subscription from 1, 000 of the 4th Duke of Northumberland's tenants after he lowered rents by 25% during a period of agricultural depression. Unfortunately the rent was raised soon after the column was built and it became known as the 'farmers folly'.

Dolly Peel, River Drive, South Shields,

Dorothy Peel was a 19th century heroine who helped men evade press gangs. She was involved in the smuggling of tobacco, perfume, lace and other goods.

Art Galleries

Baltic, Gateshead Quays

Formerly a disused 1950s grain warehouse it is now a 3,000 sq m used for contemporary visual art.

Biscuit Factory, Newcastle

The biggest single commercial art space in the UK.

Buddle Arts Centre, Wallsend

Home of the AdHoc Gallery.

Colliers, Newcastle

A large selection of paintings and prints with particular emphasis on local scenes.

Gateshead Library Gallery

A forum for local artists and touring exhibitions.

Globe City, Newcastle

Aims to be cool and cutting edge.

Hatton Gallery, University of Newcastle

Home of the internationally famous 'Schwitters' Merzbarn', which Channel 4 described as 'the seminal piece of 20th century British art'. The gallery also hosts temporary exhibitions.

Art

The Laing, Newcastle

Paintings by Lowry, John Martin, the Cullercoats school plus silver, glass and pottery. Excellent for children and people with a serious interest in art.

Queens Hall, Hexham

Regular exhibitions throughout the year.

Shipley Art Gallery, Gateshead

Also the home of a museum. Strong on textiles, glass, ceramics, jewellery and furniture.

University Gallery, University of Northumbria

Hosts temporary and touring exhibitions, they are not afraid to be adventurous.

Waygood, Newcastle

Located in an old warehouse in the heart of Newcastle, the building is also home for a large number of artists who rent studio space.

Literature

There are many writers whose have their roots in Tyneside and Northumberland, many writers who have settled in the area and also many writers who have been inspired by the area. The 'Centre for The Childrens Book', is a national resource is based in Newcastle.

Viz

A publishing phenomenon created by Chris Donald with the help of his brother. When the magazine was started in 1979 it was sold in pubs and student unions'. At its peak a 'Top 10' selling magazine, it must be the only product that proudly markets itself as "not as good as it used to be".

One may have thought that Chris Donald, as a child, would have read the *Beano* every week, rather than *Look and Learn*. It is interesting to note that many of the illustrations in '*Look and Learn*' were created by Ronald Embleton, famous for his art work depicting Roman latrines. If he had read the *Beano*, Chris Donald may not have developed his lavatorial humour!

The name *Viz* was apparently chosen because the letters V, I and Z were the easiest to carve out from cork tiling (the first issues were printed using a printing set made from Chris Donald's Dad's cork tiles).

Viz Characters

A number of stories circulate regarding the inspiration for Viz characters, so it is difficult to be absolute.

One does not have to look far to see where the idea for *Biffa Bacon* came from. Mind you, *Biffa* is as soft as clarts compared to *Mutha* (no one is 'harder' than *Mutha*).

It has been suggested that the *Fat Slags* were based on a couple of ladies observed on a night out in Nottingham, (which would make sense, as quite clearly ladies from Tyneside and Northumberland are far too cultured and fragrant) however women on the Bigg Market have also been mentioned as the inspiration (must be from elsewhere in the country, visiting for a hen night out).

Roger Mellie - the Man on the Tellie is a consummate professional apparently based on a presenter who was regularly seen in the pub opposite Tyne Tees TV (possibly the Rose and Crown - now demolished) whose behaviour completely contradicted his on screen persona.

Parkie the Park Keeper is based on a park keeper who used to shout at Chris Donald as he walked home from school across Jesmond Dene.

Sid the Sexist apparently is based on a friend of the writing team.

Authors

There have been hundreds of acclaimed writers from the region covering all genres: childrens, adult, literary, romantic, thrillers and many books that document life in the region.

The M.A. in Creative Writing at Northumbria University should ensure that there will be many new writers in the future.

David Almond

He grew up in Felling and has become one of Britain's leading writers for children. His first children's novel *Skellig* won the Whitbread prize and the Carnegie medal.

Gordon Burn

A well respected contemporary writer, he has written about 'true crime' and his critically acclaimed novels include *Alma Cogan* and *The Home Service*.

Chaz Brenchley

Chaz is a prolific writer of crime, thrillers and murder novels, he won 'Northern Writer of Year' 2000 and lives in Newcastle.

Elinor Brent-Dyer

A prolific children's writer, born in South Shields in 1894. Her *Chalet School* series sold more than 150,000 copies annually for many years.

Thomas Callaghan

Writer of Geordie classic *A Lang Way To The Pawnshop* depicting life in 1930s Tyneside, which was followed by a number of books about his life and travels.

Sid Chaplin

Sid moved to Newcastle from Shildon in 1957. Arguably his most critically acclaimed novels are *The Day of The Sardine* and *The Watcher and The Watched* set in the working-class communities of Scotswood, Elswick and Byker.

Carol Clewlow

Her *Woman's Guide to Adultery* is now a Virago modern classic. Now teaches at the University of Northumbria.

Jack Common

Writer of Geordie classics *Kiddars Luck* and *The Ampersand*. Born in Heaton, Newcastle and is buried in Newport Pagnell.

Catherine Cookson

Jarrow born, she is a publishing phenomenon; an international best seller and the most borrowed author from libraries.

She has received the ultimate accolade from South Tyneside which markets itself as 'Cookson Country'.

Julia Darling

Born in Winchester in the house in which Jane Austen died, she has been based in Newcastle for many years. Both *Crocodile Soup* and *The Taxi Driver's Daughter* have achieved critical success.

Janet MacLeod Trotter

Born in Newcastle, she now lives in Northumberland and has written a number of books set in the North -East. Two recent novels have been based on Catherine Cookson's life: *The Jarrow Lass* and *A Child of Jarrow*.

Jack Higgins

He was born in Newcastle and also published under his real name Harry Patterson, writer of international best sellers including *The Eagle Has Landed*.

Harry Pearson

Based in Northumberland, Harry has written a number of successful books including *The Far Corner* and *Racing Pigs and Giant Marrows*. He also has a column in the Guardian.

Jonathan Tulloch

A Gateshead teacher, he wrote *The Season Ticket* (which was turned into the film *Purely Belta*). This was followed up by *The Bonny Lad*.

Robert Westall

His *The Machine Gunners* won the Carnegie medal and became a popular children's television serial.

Authors that have been influenced by Tyneside and Northumberland

John Braine

Room At the Top may not have been based in this region, but the author worked on his novel at Newbiggin library where he was employed.

G.K. Chesterton

The Father Brown story *The Worst Crime In The World* was set in Bamburgh castle.

Daniel Defoe

Apparently wrote *Robinson Crusoe* whilst staying in Gateshead.

The George, Chollerford

W.H. Auden and John Steinbeck have both stayed at the George Hotel.

J.B. Priestley

During the First World War in late 1915 he was stationed at Tynemouth.

Sir Walter Scott

He wrote part of *Rob Roy* in the Rose and Thistle Inn in Alwinton. The siege of Norham Castle features in Scott's poem Marmion,

Yeugeni Zamyatin

An engineer, he was sent to England by the Russian government to supervise the building of ice breakers for the navy. He wrote *We*, the first anti-utopia. The book contains many references to working practices in Tyneside shipyards. *We* is considered to have influenced Aldous Huxley's *Brave New World* and George Orwell who read it in French before writing *1984*.

Poets

Beowulf

The first major poem written in a European vernacular language, originated in Northumbria in the 7th or early 8th century.

Basil Bunting

The first and principal British modernist poet was born at 258 Denton Road in what was then Scotswood-on-Tyne.

Playwrights & Scriptwriters

Probably the highest profile script writer is Ian La Frenais, responsible with Dick Clement for; *The Likely Lads, Porridge, Auf Wiedersehen, Pet* and many film scripts including work on *James Bond* films.

Many television drama series and soap operas use script writers from Tyneside and Northumberland. Steve Chambers has contributed to *Casualty, Byker Grove* and many others. Michael Chaplin (son of Sid) originated *Monach of the Glen*. Peter Dillon has written for *Emmerdale* as well as a number of films. Karen Young has also written for *Emmerdale*.

A number of playwrights have based plays and film scripts in the region; Peter Flannery wrote *Our Friends In The North,* Tom Hadaway has received critical acclaim for his plays based on the North Shields fishing industry. Lee Hall wrote the blockbuster *Billy Elliot*. Alan Plater has been a prolific playwright over many years and still writes plays relating to Tyneside. C.P. Taylor wrote *And A Nightingale Sang,* a bitter-sweet comedy set in wartime Tyneside, the Tyne Tees TV production of which won a Prix Europa.

Film, Television, Cinema & Entertainers

Actors

There has been a tradition of fine actors from the region. In recent years the Live Theatre has been and continues to be the starting point for many thespians.

Rowan Atkinson

Star of *Not The Nine O'Clock News*, *Blackadder*, *Thin Blue Line*, *Mr Bean* and a number of film roles.

Libby Davison

Best known for playing WDC Liz Rawton in *The Bill*, she has appeared on stage regularly particularly at the Live Theatre.

Jack Douglas

Best known as a member of the 'Carry-On' team, Jack has played numerous serious and comic parts.

Billy Fane

Actor, author and poet. Noted for his roles in *Byker Grove* and *Billy Elliot*.

Robson Green

Northumberland born, Robson has appeared in *Casualty*, *Soldier, Soldier*, *The Grafters* and many, many other one-off dramas and series.

Tim Healy

First found fame in *Auf Wiedersehen, Pet*, Tim has gone on to achieve critical acclaim for many roles on television and stage.

Eric Idle

Forever famous as a member of the Monty Python team, he was born in South Shields.

Jimmy Nail

His first major role was *Oz* in *Auf Wiedersehen, Pet*, he went on to star in *Spender* and *Crocodile Shoes*.

Imogen Stubbs

The Rothbury born actress is best known for playing private detective *Anna Lee*. She made her name with the R.S.C.

Dame Flora Robson

From South Shields, she appeared in more than 60 films. Flora Robson is one of Britain's greatest ever actresses.

Bill Travers

Not only noted for his long and distinguished acting career, but also for his work as a conservationist. Most famous for his role in *Born Free*.

Denise Welch

Star of *Soldier, Soldier* she achieved popular acclaim in one of television top character roles, landlady of *Coronation Street's* Rovers Return.

Kevin Whatley

The Peoples Theatre in Heaton was his starting point, well known for *Auf Wiedersehen, Pet, Inspector Morse, Peak Practice* plus many other starring roles.

John Woodvine

Originally from Tyne Dock, John Woodvine has been in countless television dramas and stage productions over his long acting career.

Films

Northumberland has been the location for many films over many years and continues to be popular for historical dramas. Alnwick and Bamburgh castles have appeared in more films than many leading film stars! The county provides an excellent backdrop, it is a shame that more films are not set in Northumberland.

Tyneside has recently been dubbed '*Hollywood on Tyne*', perhaps a similarity with Hollywood is that many films do not manage to make general release to cinemas nationwide.

The greatest British gangster film of all time is arguably *Get Carter*: Newcastle and Gateshead are integral to the film, perhaps the most famous scene is where Michael Cain throws Alf Roberts off Gateshead's multi-storey car park. *Purely Belta* has received critical acclaim and is probably one of the best comedy dramas set in contemporary Britain in recent years.

Probably the most famous film directors from the region are two brothers, Ridley Scott born in South Shields and Tony Scott born in North Shields.

Great films made in Tyneside and Northumberland

* Alien III

* Becket

* Cul de Sac

* El Cid

* Get Carter

* Harry Potter and the Sorcerers' Stone

* Harry Potter and the Prisoner of Azaban

* Mary Queen of Scots

* Macbeth

* Robin Hood Prince of Thieves

* Payroll

* Purely Belta

* The Spaceman and King Arthur

* Stormy Monday

* Women in Love

Television

There have been many television programmes that have been located in the region. For many of the programmes, Tyneside and Northumberland has been integral to the story. The use of a lead character from London or somewhere 'down south' has perhaps, on occasion followed the use of a token American lead in British films of the 50s and 60s (*Spender*, *550 North*, *See You Friday*).

Auf Wiedsersehen, Pet used characters from Tyneside and Northumberland, featuring locations all over the world.

Ten Great Television Series

*   Auf Wiedersehen, Pet

*   Badger

*   Byker Grove

*   Crocodile Shoes

*   550 North

*   The Likely Lads/Whatever Happened To The Likely Lads

*   Spender

*   Supergran

*   Our Friends In The North

*   When The Boat Comes In

Ten Broadcasters

Donna Air

Presenter of *The Big Breakfast* and a *Byker Grove* alumnus.

Declan Joseph Donnelly

Best known as 'Dec'. Started on *Byker Grove*, currently one half of the country's 'top light entertainment partnership'.

William Hardcastle

His career in journalism started on the North Shields *Evening News*, he went on to edit the Daily Mail and then moved into broadcasting, working on Radio 4's *World at One* and *P.M.*

Bob Johnson

Tyne Tees weatherman, well loved for his unusual weather language and knowledge of climate records going back over many centuries.

Carol Malia

The *Look North* anchor hails from Cullercoats and has won a national award for her performance as a regional news programme presenter.

Mike Neville MBE

A presenter of local news from the days when owning a television was a novel introduction to the household. He continues to keep the people of the region up to date with 'news, events and happenings'.

Anthony David McPartlin

Best known as 'Ant' started on *Byker Grove*, currently one half of the country's 'top light entertainment partnership'.

Brian Redhead

Presenter of Radio 4's *Today* programme 1975 - 1993

Miriam Stoppard

Popular television doctor and presenter of *Where The Heart Is*.

Sid Waddel

The academic turned darts commentator was born in Alnwick.

Tyne Tees

When Tyne Tees Television was formed it was nearly called North-East TV, but it was thought this might sound a bit like 'nettie' which clearly would be inappropriate. Another name considered was Tyne Wear and Tees TV. Clearly if the Wear was to be included for completeness it would be necessary to include the Tweed; that would have made a company name difficult to pronounce. It started broadcasting on the January 15th 1959.

A number of programmes have been made for the national ITV network by TyneTees.

Music programmes; *The Geordie Scene*, *Razzmatazz,* and *The Tube* which was broadcast on Channel 4 on Friday tea times from 1982 - 1987.

Daytime TV; *Chainletters* and *Crosswits*.

Catherine Cookson; starting with *The Fifteen Streets* in 1989, more than a dozen adaptations have followed. They are usually dramatised in three parts.

Tyne Tees Evening News Programmes

*	1959 - 1964	North East Roundabout
*	1964 - 1969	North East Newsview
*	1969 - 1976	Today at Six
*	1976 - 1972	Northern Life
*	1993- 1993	Tyne Tees Today
*	1993 - 1999	Network North
*	1999 -	North East Tonight

Entertainers & Comedians

Bobby Thompson

The 'Little Waster' is considered by some to be the finest comedian that the north-east has ever seen. He was a phenomenon on the club circuit, he had a heavy Geordie accent and his comedy related to traditional Tyneside life.

Bobby Pattinson

The region's number one cabaret entertainer and comedian. He has entertained audiences around the world, but has been best appreciated in the north-east.

Ross Noble

From Cramlington, he has become a big star in what in the 80s would have been alternative comedy, but is now mainstream television fare.

Music

Traditional Music

Northumberland is the only county that has an instrument named after it. The Northumbrian Pipes are more closely related to French small pipes than bagpipes; the design is relatively recent compared to many pipes and dates from the mid-18th century. They are designed to be played indoors. It is probably due to Northumbrian Pipes that Northumberland has had an unbroken musical tradition.

Particular credit needs to be given to the efforts of Will Atkinson, Joe Hutton and Will Taylor for keeping traditional music alive when it was not fashionable to be interested in 'roots' music.

For many the best place to enjoy folk music is in a pub with traditional beer. *The Bridge Hotel* Newcastle is believed to be the home of Britain's longest running folk club. *The Cumberland* Byker has frequent folk music sessions. The *Tap and Spile* in Hexham and Morpeth regularly have traditional Northumbrian music.

Rapper dancing is the traditional form of folk dance with a number of active 'teams' in the area. Do not refer to them as 'morris dancers'.

The theme music (Trumpet Hornpipe) for 'Captain Pugwash' was recorded in a front room in Harbottle by Tommy Edmondson.

Ten Traditional Musicians

* *Alistair Anderson* - former High Level Ranter, accordion player

* *Will Atkinson* - mouth organ

* *Johnny Handel* - resurected the High Level Ranters

* *Joe Hutton*- piper

* *Nancy Kerr* (+ James Fagin) they have been described as the Richard and Judy of folk

* *Sandra Kerr* - the voice and guitar behind Bagpuss

* *Billy Pigg* - Considered by some to be the ultimate Northumbrian piper

* *Will Taylor* - fiddle player

* *Kathryn Tickell* - Northumbrian piper, international superstar!

* *George Welch* - singer, songwriter and comedian

The music for Auld Lang Syne was composed by William Shield from Swalwell.

The Blues

The Blues has enjoyed huge popularity in Tyneside and Northumberland since the late 50s/early 60s.

The Jumping and Hot Club, Newcastle, has staged many blues festivals over the years and brought blues stars from across the world to Tyneside. A number of pubs regularly stage blues gigs: Barrels-Berwick, Sports and Social Club-Blaydon, Magnesia Bank-North Shields, The Tyne-Newcastle.

Ten Stars and Bands From The Tyne Delta

Big Ray and the Hip Thrusters - hard rocking electric blues

Busk - soulful Ted Hawkins style blues

Deacon Jones and the Sinners - irreverent jazzy-ska- blues

Gypsy Dave - from Newcastle, Aus. to the No. 1 Newcastle, bottleneck slide blues

Johnny D - accoustic folk rootsy blues

Martin Fletcher - blues harp 21st century urban blues

Hokum Hotshots - good time party blues

Hot Licks Cookies - internationally renowned old time blues

Ray Stubbs - one man superband, leader of the R & B Allstars

No Time For Jive - harmonica led swinging blues

Popular Music

Ten Pop and Rock Musicians

Eric Burdon - Walker born former singer with the Animals

Chas Chandler - Animals' bass player he then went into music management

Bryan Ferry - studied art at Newcastle University then went on to front Roxy Music

Brian Johnson - from Dunston to lead singer with the world's top hard rock band AC/DC

Mark Knopfler - brought up in Gosforth one of the world's top rock guitarists

Hank Marvin - much imitated Shadows guitarist from Newcastle

John Miles - hard-working musician from Jarrow, worked with Tina Turner and Joe Cocker

Alan Price - a Jarrow lad who first came to fame with the Animals

Sting - Wallsend's most famous son

Neil Tennant - formed the Pet Shop Boys

Many people are surprised to learn that Jimi Hendrix used to live in Heaton, Newcastle.

Trevor Horn, record producer was born in Newcastle in 1949.

Groups

The Fifties

The fifties was the era of Rock and Roll, many consider *The Shadows* to be Britain's best ever Rock and Roll band which was formed by two lads from Newcastle: Hank Marvin and Bruce Welch.

The Sixties

The foremost group of the sixties was *The Animals* who had a number of hits and succeeded in America. The Newcastle equivalent of Liverpool's 'Cavern Club' was the 'Club A-Go-Go'. The *Junco Partners* started in the sixties and are still going.

The Seventies

Lindisfarne enjoyed huge commercial and critical success. 'Fog On The Tyne' was the best selling album of 1971. Band members over the years included: Rod Clements, Marty Craggs, Steve Daggat, Alan Hull, Ray Jackson, Ray Laidlaw and Billy Mitchell. After the sad death of Alan Hull, the band was never to be the same again. They retired in autumn 2003. Their Christmas concerts were a legend.

Dire Straits led by Mark Knopfler, brought Cullercoats and Whitley Bay to the nation's attention in the late seventies.

During the punk era *The Angelic Upstarts* from South Shields achieved chart success. They were one of the biggest names in punk.

The Eighties

The Pet Shop Boys were formed by Neil Tennant who learnt much about stagecraft whilst attending youth theatre workshops at the Peoples Theatre.

Newcastle based *Kitchenware Records* achieved national success with a number of artistes and bands including; Martin Stephenson and the Daintees, The Kane Gang, and Prefab Sprout.

The Nineties

'The Riverside' had become the music scene's focal point. *Dubstar* achieved critical and commercial success.

The Lighthouse Family achieved international acclaim. Formed by Paul Tucker and Tunde Baiyewu they released three popular albums, *Ocean Drive, Postcards From Heaven* and *Whatever Gets You Through The Day*.

The Millennium

Cheryl Tweedy, a member of *Girls Aloud* who had huge success with *Sound of the Underground*. Michelle Heaton achieved chart success with *Liberty X* a group who were runners-up in ITV's Pop Stars television programme.

Cushie Butterfield

by George Ridley

I's a broken heated keel man and I's owner heed in luv,

Wiv a young lass in Gateshead and I caal hor me duv;

Hor nam'es Cushie Butterfield and she sells Yalla clay,

And her cousin is a muckman and they caall 'him Tom Gray.

Chorus:

She's a big lass an' a bonnine lass an' she likes hor beer,

An' they caal hor Cushie Butterfield,

an' I wish she was here.

Her eyes are like two holes in a blanket burnt throo,

An' her brows in a morning wad spyen a young coo,

An ' when Aa heer hor shootin' - "Will ye buy any clay?"

Like a Candyman's trumpet, it steels my young heart away.

Chorus

Music

YE'LL oft see hor doon at Sandgate when the fresh herring cums in,

She's like a bagfull o' saadust tied round wiv a string;

She weers big goloashes tee, an' hor stockings once were white,

An' hor bedroom it's laelock, an hor hat's nivver straight.

Chorus

When I asked her to marry us, she started to laff;

"Noo, nyen o' your monkey tricks, for I like nee sic cahff"

Then she started a' bubblin' an' roared like a bull,

An' the cheps on the Keel ses I's nowt but a fooll.

Chorus

SHE says,

the chap that gets us ' ill have te work ivvery day,

An' when he's comes hyem at neets he'll heh to gan an' seek clay;

An' when he's away seekin't Aa'll myek baals an' sing,

O weel may the keel row that ma laddie's in.

She's a big, etc.

Now, I hear she has another chap, an' he hews at Shipcote,

If I thought she wad deceive me, aw'd sure cut me throat,

Aa'll doon the river sailing, an' sing "Aw'm afloat,"

Biddin adoo te Cushee Buterfield an the chap at Shipcote.

The Keel Row

Traditional

As I came through Sandgate, through Sandgate, through Sandgate,
As I came through Sandgate, I heard a lassie sing,

Chorus: Weel may the keel row, the keel row, the keel row,
Weel may the keel row, that my laddies in

Oh, wha's like my Johnnie, Sae leish, sae blithe, sae bonny?
He's foremost 'mang the Mony keel lads o' coaly Tyne.

Chorus

He'll set and row sae tightly, Or in the dance sae sprightly
He'll cut and shuffle sightly 'tis true - were he not mine.

Chorus

He wears a blue bonnet, blue bonnet, blue bonnet,
He wears a blue bonnet and a dimple in his chin;

An ' weel may the keel row, the keel row, the keel row,
Weel may the keel row, that my laddies in.

The Blaydon Races

by George Ridley

I went to Blaydon Races,
'twas on the ninth if June,
Eighteen hundred and sixty two,
On a summer's afternoon,
I took the bus from Balmbra's,
And she was heavy laden,
Away we went along Collingwood Street,
That's on the road to Blaydon.

Chorus

O lads, ye should only seen us gannin,
We passed the folks upon the road
just as they wor stannin;
There wor lots o' lads an' lasses there,
all with smiling faces,
Gan along the Scotswood Road to see the Blaydon races.

We flew past Armstrong's factory,

Music

and up to the Robin Adair,

Just gan doon to the railway bridge

the bus wheel flew off there.

The lasses lost their crinolines off,

an' the veils that hide their faces.

An' I got two black eyes an' a broken nose in ganin te Blaydon Races

Chorus

When we gat the wheel put on,

away we went again,

But them that had their noses broke,

they came back ower hyem.

Some went to the dispensary, an'others to Doctor Gibb's,

An' some sought out the Infirmary,

to mend their broken ribs.

Chorus

Now when we gat to Paradise,

Thor wes bonny gam begun,

There was four-and-twenty on the bus,

man, how they danced an' sung;

They called on me to sing a sang,

I sung them "Paddy Fagin."

I danced a jig an' swung my twig that day I went to Blaydon.

Chorus

We flew across the Chain Bridge reet into Blaydon toon,

The bellman he was calling there,

they call him Jackey Brown,

I saw him talkin' to some chaps,

and then he was persuading,

To gan an' see Geordie Ridley's concert,

in the Mechanics Hall at Blaydon.

Chorus

The rain it poured all the day,

an' made the ground quite muddy,

Coffy Johnny had a white hat on - they wor shouting

"whe stole the cuddy."

There was spice stalls an' monkey shows,

Music

an' auld wives selling ciders,
An' a chap wiv a happeny roundabout,
shouting now, me boys, for riders

Chorus

Byker Hill

If I had a penny I would have another gill,
I would have the fiddler play
The Bonny Lass of Byker Hill

Chorus: Byker Hill and Walker Shore
The collier lads for ever more
Byker Hill and Walker Shore
The collier lads for ever more

The pitman and the keelman trim
They drink bumble made from gin
Then dance they do begin
To the tune of Elsie Marley

Chorus

When I first came to the dirt I only had
but one putshirt
Now I've gotten two or three
Walker Pits done well by me

Music

Chorus

Geordie Charleton had a pig he hit
it with a shovel and it seame a jig
All the way to Duncans rig
To the tune of Elsie Marley

Chorus

Food & Drink

Eating Out

Food Centres

*   Asian - Ocean Road, South Shields

*   Chinese - Stowell Street, Newcastle

*   Fish and Chips - North Shields

*   Italian - Bigg Market area, Newcastle

It is now possible to eat cuisine from all over the globe without leaving Tyneside and Northumberland. If people wish to make their own Asian recipes the ingredients can be sourced in the west end of Newcastle, Chinese ingredients may be sourced from Stowell Street, Newcastle.

Recipes

Local recipes would be taught and handed down from mother to daughter. So clearly families would adapt the recipes, and anyway recipes would often be 'adjusted' to make use of what was available from the larder.

Stottie Bread

A stottie is described by the 'Flour Advisory Bureau' as:

"A large round bap from the north-east of England. The Geordie stottie has a fluffy texture."

Stotties can be wholemeal, white, granary, or indeed how ever you prefer your bread.

The traditional stottie filling is ham and pease pudding.

The general guidance is:

1 Use a standard bread dough recipe or recipe of your choice.

2 Use a baking tray instead of a loaf tin.

3 Bake as a huge bun (following the cooking time for the dough mix) they should be between 1 and 2 inches thick

Singing Hinnies

The high fat content, creates appetising sizzling sounds as they cook hence the name 'singing hinnies'. Originally they would have been cooked on a griddle over an open fire. Traditionally in the 19th century and earlier, a griddle was regularly used for a number of recipes. In a modern kitchen if you do not have a griddle, just use a heavy frying pan instead.

Ingredients

250 gm of plain flour

50 gm. butter

50 gm lard

25 gm of currants

1 teaspoon of baking powder

½ teaspoon salt

milk and sour cream

Method

1 Mix the fat with the flour and

2 Add the other ingredients.

3 Mix until the dough becomes soft by adding milk and sour cream.

3 Roll out and bake on both sides on a griddle.

Carlings

It is traditional to serve carlings on the Sunday before Palm Sunday. Alternative names for carlings are; maple peas, black peas, brown badgers and pigeon peas. There are a number of variations on the following recipe

Method

1 Soak overnight.

2 Boil up to an hour, depending on how soft you prefer them.

3 Fry with a little butter and salt.

4 Add vinegar, wait until the vinegar evaporates and then serve.

Leek Pudding

A form of suet pudding often served with stew.

100 gm self raising flour

50 gm suet

1 leek

A pinch of salt

Method

1 Mix flour, suet and add a pinch of salt.

2 Roll out the pastry.

3 Chop/slice the leak.

4 Put the leek inside the pastry and roll up.

5 Place in a cloth, or wrap in foil.

6 Immerse in boiling water and boil for about two hours.

Beer & Breweries

Ralph Gardner was an early brewer who established his brewery in North Shields in the 17th century. From the Middle Ages until the end of the 19th century trade around the banks of the Tyne was controlled by the Freemen of Newcastle. The Freeman claimed that Ralph was acting illegally under a clause from Queen Elizebeth's Charter, took him to court and imposed a fine of over £900 (he only had £20) then flung him into gaol. He campaigned against the ruling, published a pamphlet 'England's Grievance Discovered In Relation To The Coal Trade', which was an indictment of the Corporation of Newcastle. Sadly, Ralph ended up leaving the north-east.

Fortunately, since the early 1980s a number of fine micro breweries have formed in Tyneside and Northumberland. A number have won national awards from the Campaign for Real Ale at the Great British Beer Festival and many have won awards at beer festivals across Britain. Some micro-breweries have a small portfolio of beers, others have a diverse range of interesting beers.

The Tynside and Northumberland branch of the Campaign for Real Ale has been promoting real ale and pub heritage since the early 1970s. Every April they hold the biggest annual indoor party in the region, *The Newcastle Beer Festival*,which is currently held at Newcastle University Students Union, everyone over 18 is welcome.

Big Lamp, Newburn

The first micro brewery, formed in 1982 in the Summerhill area, just off Westgate Road in Newcastle. They are now located in Newburn at an old water pumping station (The Keelman).

Bitter, a session beer.

Summerhill Stout, the original location of the brewery,

Prince Bishop Ale, celebrates the fact that the region was once governed by the Prince Bishops.

Double M - brewed for the millennium.

Hadrian and Border, Ouseburn, Newcastle

Formed by the merger of Hadrian (which briefly became Four Rivers) and the Border Brewery originally based in Berwick upon Tweed.

Beers named with a Roman origin;

Vallum, Gladiator, Legion and Centurion were originally brewed by Hadrian.

Beers from the Border portfolio;

Farne Island Pale Ale, Flotsom, Secret Kingdom, Reiver's IPA, Northumbrian Gold, Rampart, and *Jetsam.*

Hexhamshire, Hexhamshire

A small family-run brewery based in the hills to the south of Hexham, the brewery tap is the Dipton Mill.

Devils Water is named after the river that joins the Tyne at Dilston, when crossing the 'Devils Water' in a carriage, train or motor car it is important to raise ones feet to prevent capture by the 'devil'.

Devils Elbow named after a waterfall on Devils Water.

Old Humbug named after brewer Geoff Brooker who some consider to be a 'grumpy old man'.

Shire Bitter named after Hexhamshire.

Whapwheasel has two derivations; a burn in Hexhamshire or, a whap is the local name for a curlew and a wysel is its whistle.

High House, Matfen

One of the regions' most recent breweries, based in converted farm buildings. The beers are named after farm sheep dogs';

Auld Hemp is named after the first dog at High House Farm and *Nel's Best* is named after the current collie.

Jarrow, Jarrow

Opened in 2002 at the Robin Hood, Jarrow. Most of their beers names have local connections;

Jarrow Bitter the standard session beer.

River Catcher, a job is the local shipyards.

Joblings Swinging Gibbet, commemorates the last person to be hung and gibbeted.

Palmers Revolution, celebrates the local shipyard.

Red Ellen, named after firebrand local M.P. Ellen Wilkinson

Venerable Bede, he was based in Jarrow.

Old Cornelius, named after the last Jarrow Marcher.

Mordue, Shiremoor

A well established micro that won Champion Beer of Britain shortly after they set up. Their beers are regularly available across Britain.

Five Bridges Bitter, first brewed when there were only five bridges crossing the Tyne between Newcastle and Gateshead.

Geordie Pride, a self-explanatory name.

Workie Ticket, an expression that is used to describe someone who makes a nuisance of themselves.

Radgie Gadgie, a term for a person who is a little wild and prone to fly off the handle.

IPA, as one would expect an India Pale Ale.

Redburn, Bardon Mill

The former Black Bull Brewery from Haltwhistle has set up in Bardon Mill, all the beer names are Latin in derivation;

Ebrius Bitter, Summus Best Bitter, Optimus Special Ale.

Wylam, Heddon-on-the-Wall

The brewery is run by two partners, John and Robin, who promote themselves as brewers of "proper beer". Many of their beers are inspired by continental beer styles.

Bitter, this is a lighter version of Rocket and has Stephenson's Rocket on the pump clip.

Bohemia, an authentic Czech recipe beer using a Czech strain of Pilsner yeast.

Gold Tankard, made with all gold ingredients developed with local beer writer Alistair Gilmore.

Hedonist, a session beer for people who perhaps are not particularly restrained.

Hoppin Mad, a very hoppy beer that is derived from a special 'Houblon Nouveau'.

Silver Ghost, originally brewed for a beer festival in the south, named after the famous car.

Summer Magic, refreshing light and refreshing summer beer.

Whistle Stop, commissioned to celebrate the Newcastle-Carlisle railway line 'Whistle Stops' pub guide.

Wit, a Belgian style wheat beer.

Public Houses of Note

In all the following public houses it is possible to enjoy traditional, high quality real ale.

Albion, Bill Quay

Owned by the Jarrow Brewery, it probably has the best view of the Tyne from the south bank.

Allum House, South Shields

Close to the ferry landing, not far from the market place.

Bacchus, High Bridge, Newcastle

A new pub just up the street from where the previous Bacchus stood.

Barrels, Berwick upon Tweed

An unusually shaped pub that has a reputation for live music.

Bodega, Westgate Road, Newcastle

Recently restored to its former glory, it has splendid glass domes.

Black Bull, Haltwhistle

Small with a low ceiling, the focal point for beer drinkers in Haltwhistle

Boathouse, Wylam

Opposite the railway station in Wylam, it has won the Northumberland pub of the year award several times.

Bridge Hotel, opposite Newcastle Keep,

Much used as a set on television programmes, music, poetry and other events are held upstairs.

Cluny, Ouseburn, Newcastle

A pub/cafe/art gallery/venue. Regularly hosts events promoted by the famous Jumping and Hot Club.

Crown Posada, Side, Newcastle

On the national inventory of architecturally interesting pubs, it has a magnificent stained glass window and beautiful wood panelling. A small, narrow pub, don't tell everybody!

Cumberland, Byker

A fine traditional pub which is a centre for traditional music and rapper dancing.

Dipton Mill, Hexhamshire

The Hexhamshire Brewery Tap, is has won awards from CAMRA and also for its food.

Duke, High Bridge, Newcastle

Formerly the Duke of Wellington, a busy city centre pub.

Free Trade, Ouseburn, Newcastle

Named after a political movement, with a splendid view of the Tyne and Newcastle-Gateshead quaysides.

John Bull Inn, Alnwick

Not only a wide range of real ales, but also a large range of Belgian bottled beer and malt whisky.

Magnesia Bank, North Shields

The 'Maggie Bank' has developed a reputation for high quality beer, food and musical entertainment.

Riverside, Mill Dam, South Shields

Close to the Customs House, it has won awards for its beer.

Robin Hood, Primrose Hill, Jarrow

The Jarrow Brewery tap also houses an Italian restaurant!

The Star, Netherton (nr. Rothbury)

One of the few pubs to be included in every edition of the ''Good Beer Guide', a unique pub.

Tap & Spile; Hexham, Morpeth and North Shields

All individual in character; they are all lively, friendly and the hub of their communities.

The Tyne, Ouseburn, Newcastle

Unusual beer garden, regular live music from local, national and international artistes.

Animals & Wildlife

Northumberland is arguably the best county in England for wildlife. It has a diversity that cannot be matched, with many rare and threatened species. Wildlife is also thriving in urban environments.

The county is particularly popular with the bird-watchers as there are many birds that migrate to Northumberland from the Arctic during the winter. Other species arrive in early spring to breed. The Farne Islands, a group of 28 islands, provide sanctuary for many sea birds; guillemot, razorbill, puffin, shag, cormorant, tern and kittiwake, along with gull and duck.

Much of the credit for the biodiversity should go to the Northumberland Wildlife Trust which is the largest charity in the region working to safeguard native wildlife. It is one of 47 Wildlife Trusts across the UK, Northumberland Wildlife Trust has campaigned for nature conservation for over 30 years. It aims to inform, educate and involve people of all ages and backgrounds in protecting their environment in the interest of wildlife and conservation. This is achieved through practical conservation activities with plenty of volunteering opportunities, schools environmental educational programmes, community projects, corporate involvement and an ongoing programme of events held throughout the year at Trust grounds, reserves and other venues across the region. The Northumberland Wildlife Trust success is due to the supported if thousands of members, including support of businesses from across the region.

Key Nature Reserves

Hauxley

Located on a beautiful stretch of Northumberland Heritage coast close to Druridge Bay, Hauxley nature reserve was previously an opencast coal mine. It has now been transformed into one of the region's premier nature reserves and is a fantastic site for bird-watching. The water, islands and reed beds attract large numbers of birds including waders and many migrants – including Bewick swan, shoveler, lapwing and purple sandpiper. The site is also home to a variety of invertebrates and amphibians such as the rare great crested newt.

Whitelee Moor

At 1,500 hectares, Whitelee Moor is the largest National Nature Reserve in England. Located adjacent to the Scottish Borders and with magnificent views of the Cheviots and across the moorland, visitors will experience the wonderful feeling of wilderness. It is a Site of Special Scientific Interest and is of European conservation importance, due to its active blanket bog and heather heaths. Notable breeding birds include merlin and stonechat whilst regular visitors include black grouse, skylark, meadow pipit, durlin, curlew, golden plover, grey wagtail, dipper and ring ouzel.

Harbottle Crags

Part of Harbottle Moors, this Site of Special Scientific Interest is an area of beautiful open moorland located close to Harbottle in North Northumberland. It features the Drake Stone, where nearby rocks have been scratched and polished by the ice sheet of the last glaciation. The peat bog at the eastern end of the lough is home to various bog flora including the carnivorous round-leaved sundew and bog myrtle. In summer, you can spot large heath butterflies and emperor moths.

Holystone North Wood and Valley

Both located within 1km of Holystone village in upper Coquetdale. The wood is a semi-natural oak woodland, an upland habitat more typical of the Lake District. Flora includes wood anemone and birds include wood warbler, tawny owl and woodcock. The wood links into a circular Forest Enterprise marked walk. The valley site includes oak woodland as well as juniper scrub, a small area of reed bed and bushes containing bog myrtle. There are also large areas of heather. As well as providing a refuge for vegetation sensitive to grazing (including juniper) this is an important site for reptiles, including adders and slow worms.

Other Reserves

Annstead Dunes

Arnold Memorial, Craster

Barrow Burn Wood

Beltingham

Big Waters

Border Mires

Bellcrag Flow

Butterburn Flow

Chirdon Head

Falstone Moss

Felicia Moss

Gowany Knowe Moss

Haining Head

Harelaw

Hawthorne

Hobbs Flow

Horse Hill

Hummel Knowe Moss

Lakes, The

Muckle Samuel's Moss

Paddaburn Moss

Pundershaw

Wedges Rigg

The Wou

Briarwood Banks

Close House Riverside

Cresswell Pond

Dougie's Pond

Druridge Pools

East Chevington

East Cramlington Pond

East Crindledykes Quarry

Fencerhill Wood

Flodden Quarry

Ford Moss

Gooses Nest Bluebell Bank

Grasslees Burn Wood

Greenlee Lough

Grindon Lough

Harbottle Crags

Hauxley

Holburn Lake & Moss

Holystone North Wood

Holystone Valley

Holywell Pond

Animals & Wildlife

Juliets Wood

Linton Lane

Little Harle Pasture

Littlemill

Mill Burn

Newsham Pond

Priestclose Wood

South Close Field

St Nicholas Park

Tony's Patch

West Fleetham

Whitelee

Williamston

Animals

Bedlington Terriers

The famous dog was originally known as the Rothberg Terrier. John Ainsley from Bedlington owned the first dog recognised and called a Bedlington Terrier. They were originally bred for hunting. One story is that Bedlington Terriers are developed from a breed of dogs used by gypsies in the Rothbury area.

Cheviot Goats

Wild goats have roamed the Cheviots for over 200 years. They are descended from domesticated goats. During the summer they roam the tops of the hills, in winter months they are forced down to the valley bottoms. The rams have horns that grow continuously and are never shed, they can reach 76 cm in length.

Cheviot Sheep

One of the oldest sheep breeds they have a dense white fleece, they are happy grazing on hills up to 3,000 ft high and are hardy enough to stay on high ground all year.

Chillingham Cattle

A unique breed they have been isolated since 1270, when Chillingham Park was enclosed.

The population size ranges between 40 and 60, it is possible to see them at Chillingham Castle.

Cuddy Duck

The eider duck is an icon of Northumberland, it has been given the nickname 'cuddy duck' after St Cuthbert.

Grey Seals

Grey seals can be seen in large numbers around the Farne Islands. Breeding takes place in October, when territorial fights and skirmishes take place, more often than not the wounds are superficial.

Otters

In recent years otter numbers have been increasing, they can be seen in the Coquet, the Rede and other rivers.

Red Kites

Introduced to suburban Gateshead, they can now be seen soaring high in the skies above the Metro Centre.

Red Squirrels

Northumberland is the last county in England where the red squirrel has a stronghold in the wild.

Water Vole

Numbers have been increasing in recent years, which is an indication of an improvement in water quality.

Societies, Clubs & Associations

There are thousands of societies, clubs and associations in Tyneside and Northumberland. Almost every national organisation will have at least one branch in Tyneside and Northumberland.

The following short list is of locally formed organisations.

The Charles Avison Society

Charles Avison is considered to be the most important English Concerto composer of the 18th century. He started subscription concerts in 1736, the first of their kind held outside London. The Charles Avison Society has recently re-established a series of concerts.

Border Stick Dressers Association

Formed in 1951 with the aim of celebrating stick dressing skills and keeping the tradition alive. The sticks were traditionally used by shepherds.

Coble and Keelboat Society

Established in 1987 to promote and preserve traditional boats native to the Northumberland coast.

Literary and Philosophical Society

One of the oldest and biggest private libraries, founded in 1793 they moved to their present purpose built building in 1825. The 'Lit and Phil' started the inter-library loan system in the 1940s.

Northumbrian Pipers Society

Formed in 1928 to promote Northumbrian Small Pipes and pipe music.

Tyne Bikes

A campaigning organisation that promotes cycling for all.

Tynedale and Newcastle District Outdoor Club

They celebrated their 50th anniversary in 2003 and are a founding member of the national naturist organisation.

Sport

Football

Newcastle United

Formed by the Merger of Newcastle West End and Newcastle East End (two clubs playing in the Northern League). The decision on the name Newcastle United was taken on December 9th 1892 at a meeting held in Bath Lane Hall. Other names proposed at the time included Newcastle City and Newcastle Rangers. Due to a legal quirk the actual name change was not sanctioned by the Board Of Trade until November 1895.

Newcastle United's first match under their new name was played on December 10th 1892 against local rivals. Newcastle lost 1-2 in front of a crowd of 2,500.

Nickname

Newcastle's Magpies nickname appeared around the end of 1895. Until then they actually played in Red and White shirts, the famous Black n White stripes only appearing in August 1894 due to numerous colour clashes with opponents whilst wearing red.

The nickname has two main sources :-

A Dominican Priest supported Newcastle United

and could be seen in his distinctive black and white habit. He was often seen associating with the players and his black and white garb led to "The Magpies" nickname.

Or

A legend has it that a pair of real magpies nested in the original Victorian stand at the ground, the players become attached to the magpies. Hence calling themselves the Magpies.

Although, nowadays newly designed football tops have narrow bands of black, many away supporters have taken to calling Newcastle United fans 'The Barcodes'.

Honours

Football League Div 1

Champions 1904-05, 1906-07, 1908-09, 1926-27, 1992-93

Football league Division 2

Champions 1964-65

Runners up 1897-98, 1947-48

Premier League

Runners up 1995-96, 1996-97

FA Cup

Winners 1910, 1924, 1932, 1951, 1952, 1955

Runners up 1905, 1906, 1908, 1911, 1974, 1998, 1999

Football League Cup

Runners up 1975

Inter-cities Fairs Cup

Winners 1968-69

Player achievements

Current players have been excluded from the list as clearly their statistics change every week. At the time of compilation the second-highest goal scorer in club history is Alan Shearer, in time he may well take the top spot from Jackie Milburn.

Most League & Cup Appearances

496 games - Jimmy Lawrence 1904-1922

472 games – Frank Hudspeth 1910-1929

457 games – Frank Clark 1962-1975

432 games – Bill McCracken 1904-1923

431 games – Alf McMichael 1949-1963

412 games – David Craig 1962-1978

408 games – Bobby Mitchell 1949-1961

Goals

Most League & Cup Goals (for Newcastle United)

200 - Jackie Milburn 1946-57

153 – Len White 1953-62

143 – Hughie Gallacher 1925-30

121 – Malcolm McDonald 1971-76

119 – Peter Beardsley 1983-97 (2 periods with club)

113 – Bobby Mitchell 1949-61

113 – Tom McDonald 1921-31

101 – Neil Harris 1920-25

97 – Bryan Robson 1962-71

Toon's lowest moments

(for the fans anyway!!)

5th December 1908

Newcastle lost 1-9 at home to local, and bitter, rivals Sunderland!!! Although the excuse was that Newcastle finished the game with 9 men due to injuries (these being in the days before substitutes).

28th April 1934

Newcastle lose 1-2 to Stoke City and end the season relegated to Division Two. Where, due to the outbreak of the 2nd World War they remain until gaining promotion in 1948.

5th February 1972

Newcastle lost 1-2 to non-league Hereford United in a 3rd round FA Cup replay at Hereford. The game was captured on television, Newcastle fans every year since have to watch endless replays of a long range volley by part-timer Ronnie Radford (he was a cab driver by trade) every time the FA Cup campaign commences.

4th May 1974

Newcastle are comprehensively outplayed by Liverpool and lose 0-3 in the FA Cup Final at Wembley. Two of the goals are scored by Kevin Keegan.

16th May 1990

Newcastle are involved in a play off against Sunderland to determine who has a chance of gaining promotion back to the First Division. The first of the two legs at Roker Park ended 0-0 following an ill-tempered game. With home advantage hopes were high. However, Sunderland won 2-0. This sparked a pitch invasion which held the end of the game up by 20 minutes. The loss was made worse when Sunderland were promoted despite losing to Swindon Town in the play-off final, as Swindon were disqualified due to a betting scandal. Newcastle had finished the season 3rd, Sunderland 6th.

The best team of all time - the dream team

This is a selection of Newcastle United's best ever 11 players, taking into account, for each player, his number of appearances for the club, how good a player he was considered in his time, the club's success and his international record while he was playing. There are players that are remembered fondly, but who didn't stay around too long (Shackleton), or really became household names when they'd moved somewhere else (Waddle, Beardsley, Gascoigne).

Newcastle has been a mediocre club for most of its' history (only a fan is permitted to make the comment). Its best times were by far in the first decade of the 20th century. It is natural that several of the "best 11" come from this period. Then there were the early 50s (3 FA Cup wins, though generally poor league form), the 26-27 season when they last won the league, and 1993 to date, with many top-6 finishes and 2 FA Cup final appearances. The team that won the Fairs Cup in 1969 did virtually nothing else.

Team formations have changed over the years, from the original 2-3-5 to the modern 4-4-2, so team positions are not always easy to compare. So, for the dream team of all time we are going to use a 4-3-3 formation, partly because it is between the two, partly because Newcastle have had more famous attacking players than defensive ones. Shirt numbers are allocated to players according to what would probably be their playing positions in a 4-3-3 line-up, this to assist in finding the best for each position:

No. 9 shirt

To start, the most coveted shirt, for which there are three candidates: Gallacher, Milburn and Shearer. Milburn is the most famous of Newcastle players and must be included. Gallacher scored 36 goals in 38 games to help Newcastle win their last ever league title, in 1927. He too is a legend and should walk into the team. Alan Shearer has been arguably the nation's best centre-forward for the last ten years, a real leader, the most expensive player in the world when Newcastle bought him. He symbolises the modern Newcastle United. So which one? Dream team manager would pick all three players, in our three-man forward line. He would give the no. 9 shirt to Shearer, as leader of the pack. Milburn would play in a wider position (he started out there), and consequently wear the no. 11 shirt. Gallacher has the no. 8 shirt, feeding off Shearer.

Goalkeeper

There are not many greats to choose from. It is between Simpson and Lawrence. Lawrence gets the vote because he is the player who played the most ever games for Newcastle, and won the most trophies, as part of the great Edwardian team.

Defence

The dream team manager is in his forties and does not remember Newcastle having much of a defence, so there's nobody from the last 30 or so years he would pick. Other than centre-half Brennan from the 50s, it would again seem that the Edwardian team provided about the best we've ever had. Hudspeth (2) and McCracken (3) would therefore be the full-backs, and Aitken would get the no. 6 shirt, "arguably United's finest pre-war player"

Midfield

With three up-front, we now need 3 "real" midfielders. There is therefore no room for Rutherford on the right, normally the best right-winger, so he will play as centre half. The selection is for a middle line of Colin Veitch (7) for his versatility, Robert Lee (10), who was a major influence during Keegan's era, and Peter McWilliam (4), to play behind Milburn on the left.

Of the eleven, five are from the very early days, two from the Gallacher period, two from the 50s cup team, and two from the Keegan/post-Keegan era. Five are Scots, there are four from the north-east, plus an Irishman and a southerner.

1 Lawrence

2 Hudspeth   5 Brennan   6 Aitken   3 McCracken

7 Veitch   10 Lee   4 McWilliam

8 Gallacher   9 Shearer   11 Milburn

Newcastle United are clearly the region's biggest club, they are the only Premier League club. Other clubs of merit include; Berwick Rangers who are the only English club to play in Scotland, Blyth Spartans who have attracted national attention on a number of occasions.

Other Players and People Connected to Newcastle of Note

Peter Beardsley played for England and was a key player during Keegan's reign

Bob Stokoe played for Newcastle and managed Sunderland

Jimmy Scoular wing half, played for Newcastle

Bobby Mitchell left winger from Scotland, Newcastle star

Ronnie Simpson, Newcastle goalkeeper, Scotland international who went on to achieve immortality with Celtic

Stan Seymour Manager of Newcastle

1939-1947 then 1950-1954 then 1956-1958

Kevin Keegan as a player and manager brought Newcastle back to greatness

Bob Moncur Scottish international centre half 296 League games for Newcastle and lifted the Fairs Cup as captain

Great Footballers from the region

So many great footballers over the history of the game have been born in Tyneside and Northumberland, it is not possible to list them all. The following list is the best of the best.

"Geordie" Armstrong left Hebburn aged 17 and made a record 621 appearances for Arsenal.

Bobby and Jackie Charlton the two brothers from Ashingtond who played for England.

Paul Gascoigne Dunston's greatest player.

Chris Waddle from Gateshead

Athletics

There is a great tradition of middle distance running with many athletics clubs and a vibrant 'Harrier League' for cross-country and road-racing. The Great North Run was launched in 1979 and is the world's biggest half-marathon.

Top Athletes

Jim Alder - marathon runner

Steve Cram - Jarrow and Hebburn

Johnathan Edwards - Gateshead

Brendon Foster - Gateshead

Mike McLeod - born in Dilston

David Sharpe - Jarrow and Hebburn

Charlie Spedding - Gateshead

Cricket

Thomas William Graveney as a test cricketer he made 11 centuries for England.

Steve Hamison is officially the best fast-bowler in the world.

Rowing

Robert Chambers was the first Tyneside sculler to become a world champion.

Harry Clasper was born in Dunston in 1812. He became world champion sculler, tens of thousands of people used to line the Tyne placing bets on him to win.

James Renforth won the sculling Championship of the World in 1868, and stroked a Tyne four to win the Championship of the World on the St Lawrence River near Montreal in 1870.

Rugby

Rob Andrew manager of Newcastle Falcons Rugby team.

Jonny Wilkinson now England Captain, England would not have been World Champions if it was not for Johnny's golden boot!

Skating

Joanne Conway was British Figure Skating Champion.

Sport

Motor Sport

Sir Frank Williams is from South Shields.

Swimmer

Chris Cooke an olympic swimmer from South Shields, he broke the British and Commowealth 100m breaststroke record in 2003.

Susan Rolph City of Newcastle Swimming Club, 1999 was her best year when her world ranking was 4th 100m freestyle, 8th 50m freestyle and 5th 200m medley.

Wind Surfing

Sam Lamiroy started at Tynemouth and has become British Champion.

Sports Venues

Athletics

Gateshead Stadium

One of the UK's top athletics stadia, many records have been broken over many years. It is the home of Gateshead Athletic Club.

Wentworth, Hexham

A recently built 'tartan' running track, it has hosted a number of international athletics meetings.

Basketball

Metro Radio Arena

Home of Newcastle Eagles.

Cricket

Northumberland Cricket Club

For many years Northumberland county matches have been held at the Jesmond Cricket ground. In recent years the ground has been over-shadowed by the new Riverside ground at Chester-le-Street.

Greyhound Racing

Brough Park, Newcastle

Busy greyhound track.

Horse Racing

Hexham

A beautiful setting, high above Hexham town. It is believed that horse racing has been held on the site since 1793.

Newcastle, Gosforth

Hosting 32 meetings a year, Newcastle Racecourse is the busiest turf track in the UK. The highlight of the year is the three day day Northumberland Plate Festival which includes the Pitman's Derby which has a history dating back to 1833 and is the richest two mile handicap in the northern hemisphere.

Ice-Hockey

Metro Radio Arena

Home of Newcastle Vipers.

Rugby League

Gateshead Stadium

Rugby League has been a recent addition at Gateshead.

Rugby Union

Kingston Park

Newcastle Falcons' ground has seen impressive development over the last few years.

Speedway

Brough Park

Newcastle Diamonds share the stadium with the greyhound track.

Shielfield Park, Berwick

Home of Berwick Bandits.

People

Freeman of Newcastle

Becoming a 'Freeman of the City of Newcastle' does not provide the recipient with grazing rights on the town moor, but it is a prestigous honour.

4 May 1977

Jimmy Carter

39th President of the United States of America.

"In recognition of his eminent services for the furtherance of friendship between nations and on the occasion of his historic visit to the City."

1 March 1978

Captain, Officers and Ship's Company of the H.M.S. "Newcastle"

"In recognition of the long association of ships of Her Majesty's Royal Navy bearing the name of the City, the names of the Captain, Officers and Ship's Company of H.M.S. "Newcastle" be placed on the Roll of Honorary Freemen of the City of Newcastle upon Tyne; that the Council confer upon the Captain, Officers and Ship's Company the privilege, honour and distinction of marching through the streets of the City on all ceremonial occasions with bayonets fixed, drums beating and colours flying."

2 January 1980

101st (Northumbrian) Field Regiment Royal Artillery (Volunteers)

"In recognition of 120 years connection with and service to the City; that the Council confers upon the Regiment the privilege, honour and distinction of marching through the streets of the City on all ceremonial occasions with bayonets fixed, colours flying and bands playing."

2 June 1982

Daisy Dorothy Clark, M.B.E.

"In recognition of her eminent and outstanding achievement in raising over £1million for the Charlie Bear Whole Body Scanner Appeal."

David Scott Cowper F.R.I.C.S.

"In recognition of his eminent and outstanding achievements in twice circumnavigating the world single handed."

25 July 1984

201 (Northern) General Hospital, Royal Army Medical Corps (Volunteers)

"In recognition of the 150th anniversary of the Medical School of the University of Newcastle upon Tyne (founded in 1834 as the School of Medicine and Surgery), many of whose officers have been graduates of the School; that the Council confer upon the Unit the privilege, honour and distinction of marching through the streets of the City on all ceremonial occasions with bands playing."

2 October 1985

Royal Naval Reserve (Tyne Division)

"In recognition of 80 years connection with and service to the City; that the Council confers upon the Division the privilege, honour and distinction of marching through the streets of the City on all ceremonial occasions with bands playing."

2 April 1986

Nelson Mandela

"In recognition of his services to the cause of freedom"

At the time the freedom was conferred upon Nelson Mandela by the City Council he was serving life imprisonment in South Africa. The original

Freedom Scroll was received on his behalf by Mr. Ralph Mzamo, a representative of the African National Congress during an A.N.C. Rally in Newcastle upon Tyne on Saturday 4th October 1986. Following Nelson Mandela's release from prison in 1991 he was subsequently elected President of South Africa. During a visit to the United Kingdom in 1993 at a joint ceremony in the City Hall, Glasgow, together with other British local authorities who had also conferred the honour upon him, Nelson Mandela was presented with a substitute Freedom Scroll by the then Lord Mayor of Newcastle upon Tyne, Councillor Mrs. Joan Lamb.

Andrei Sakharov

"In recognition of his services to the cause of freedom."

30 April 1986

Bob Geldof

"In recognition of his eminent and outstanding work in initiating financial and practical measures for Third World famine relief not only by personal effort but by raising national awareness of the severe plight and needs of underdeveloped countries."

5 July 1989

The Royal Marines

"In recognition since 1664 of their true and loyal service in which Corps many distinguished men of

Newcastle upon Tyne, including Lord Collingwood, have served (and in particular recognising the service to the City of Royal Marines Reserve Tyne); that the Council confers upon the Royal Marines the privilege, honour and distinction of marching through the streets of the City on all ceremonial occasions with bayonets fixed, colours flying and bands playing."

St. John Ambulance Northumbria

"In recognition of their outstanding service to the local community for over 100 years and their continuing commitment to the provision of voluntary medical care in the future."

1 July 1992

Lord Taylor of Gosforth

The Lord Chief Justice of England

"In recognition of his eminent and outstanding achievements."

26 May 1993

Newcastle United Football Club

"In recognition of over 100 years sporting achievement in the Football League and F.A.Cup and European competitions and of the Club's contribution to the reputation of the City and its place in the hearts of Geordies everywhere."

5 April 1995

Councillor Sir Jeremy Hugh Beecham, M.A., D.C.L.

"In recognition of eminent and outstanding service rendered to the City for 17 years as leader of the City Council during the period May 1977 to December 1994."

1 October 1997

Royal Shakespeare Company

"In recognition of their outstanding contribution to the cultural life of the City and the Region through their association with the Theatre Royal over the last 21 years."

1 April 1998

Councillor Theresa Science Russell, O.B.E., D.C.L.,J.P.

"In recognition of 50 years eminent and outstanding public service rendered to the City."

2 February 2000

To Mark the Start of the New Millennium

"This Council in pursuance of the provisions of the Local Government Act 1977 hereby confers upon those babies born in Newcastle on the 1st day of

January 2000 the Honorary Freedom ot the City of Newcastle upon Tyne"

Harriet Jean Dunlop, Dillan Richard Horsburgh, Nathan Lee Douglas, Lewis John White, Kieran Paul Crump, Jordan Rose Nicholson, Rachel Isobel Somerville

6 December 2000

The Rt. Hon. Nicholas Hugh Brown MP

"In recognition of his eminent and outstanding public service as a former Member of Newcastle City Council, former parliamentary Secretary to the Treasury and currently as Cabinet Member and Minister of Agriculture, Fisheries and Food."

The Rt. Hon. Lord Glenamara CH (Ted Short)

"In recognition of his eminent and outstanding public service as former Member of Newcastle City Council, former MP for Newcastle Central Constituency, former Parliamentary Secretary to the Treasury and Deputy Prime Minister and currently Chancellor of the University of Northumbria at Newcastle."

The Sage Group PLC

"In recognition of their position as the Region's only FTSE 100 company and for their contribution to the economic regeneration of the City."

Alan Shearer

"In recognition of his role as Captain of Newcastle United Football Club and as former Captain of England which have enhanced the reputation of the City."

Jonathan Edwards, CBE

"In recognition of his sporting achievements including winning a gold medal at the Sydney Olympic Games which have raised national interest in athletics as well as enhancing the reputation of the City."

3 December 2003

Jonny Wilkinson

"In recognition of his sporting achievements and in particular, the key role which he has played in England's Rugby World Cup success in Australia, enhancing the reputation of the City and the country."

Freemen of Gateshead

There are five people who have been awarded the freedom of the Borough of Gateshead.

1978

Sister Winifred Laver

Father Bernard Aloysius Strong

People

2002

Jonathan Edwards
George Gill

2004

Brendan Foster

Freemen of South Shields

Richard Annand

Second Lieutenant Annand was the member of the Army to win the Victoria Cross in the Second World War. He was serving with the Durham Light Infantry, by the River Dyle, south-east of Brussels on 16 May 1940. The platoon he was commanding fought against a German attack on a bridge that been destroyed by British forces. When ammunition ran out, he ran forward over open ground, under heavy fire, and drove the enemy away with hand grenades. He was wounded, but after having his wounds dressed he resumed command, and went forward alone again inflicting heavy casualties with grenades. Following the withdrawl of his platoon, he discovered his batman was missing. Second Lieutenant Annand went back to the thick of the battle and brought the batman back in a wheelbarrow, before losing consciousness as a result of his wounds. He was presented with his Victoria Cross by King George VI in September 1940.

Catherine Cookson - Honoured in the seventies,

Boats, Planes, Trains & Bicycles

Port of Tyne Authority

Approximately 850,00 passengers pass through the Port of Tyne every year. Cruise ships also operate from the port.

Scheduled passenger sailings

Destination	Country	Line	Frequency
Amsterdam (Ijmuiden)	Netherlands	DFDS	daily
Gothenburg	Sweden	DFDS	2 a week
Kristiansand	Sweden	DFDS	2 a week
Bergen Haugesund Stavanger	Norway	Fjord	3 a week

Scheduled container sailings.

Destination	Frequency
Felixstowe	2 a week
Grangemouth	3 a week
Rotterdam	2 a week

Newcastle International Airport

The airport's baggage handlers handle 2.5 million suitcases each year.

Over 50 tour operators fly to 43 destinations on charter flights for holidays.

Direct Services

Destination	Airline
Aberdeen	Eastern Airways
Alicante	easyJet
Amsterdam	KLM
Barcelona	easyJet
Belfast	easyJet/Flybe British European
Berlin	easyJet
Birmingham	Eastern Airways
Bristol	easyJet
Brussels	SN Brussels Airlines
Budapest	easyJet
Cardiff	Air Wales
Copenhagen	SAS Scandanavian Airlines/easyJet
Dublin	Ryanair
Dusseldorf	Lufthansa
Exeter	Flybe British European
Geneva	easyJet

Travel

Hanover	Hapag-Lloyd Express
Isle of Man	Eastern Airways
London Gatwick	British Airways
London Heathrow	British Airways
London Stanstead	easyJet
Malaga	easyJet
Nice	easyJet
Palma Mallorca	easyJet
Paris Charles De Gaulle	Air France/easyJet
Plymouth	Air Wales
Prague	easyJet
Rome	easyJet
Southampton	Eastern Airways/Flybe British European
Stavanger	Wideroe

Great North Eastern Railway

It takes about three hours to reach London Kings Cross from Newcastle, the fastest journey is on the Flying Scotsman service.

GNER also serves Morpeth, Alnmouth and Berwick-upon-Tweed and continues north as far as Inverness.

Stations served by principal GNER services

Glasgow Central, Edinburgh, Durham, Darlington,

Northallerton, York, Doncaster, Retford, Newark, Grantham, Peterborough, Stevenage and Kings Cross.

Virgin Cross-Country

Virgin runs trains via Birmingham New Street to the south coast (Southampton, Bournemouth) and the south west (Bristol, Exeter, Plymouth, Penzance). Trains depart for the south twice an hour during much of the day. It is quicker to travel via Doncaster instead of Leeds and Wakefield to Birmingham.

Cycling

The principal touring circuit of Northumberland utilises three sections of the National Cycle Network (NCN).

Coast & Castles Cycle Route (NCN 1)

From Tyneside the route follows the Northumberland coastline to Berwick-upon-Tweed and then along the route of the Tweed.

Pennine Cycleway (NCN 68)

From the Tweed through the Cheviots, through the fringes of Kielder Forest to Haltwhistle.

Hadrian Cycleway (NCN 72)

The route follows the route of Hadrian's Wall and the Tyne.

Coast2 Coast

A popular and arduous route, most people cycle west to east starting in Whitehaven and cycling the 140 miles to Tynemouth.

Mileage from Newcastle

Aberdeen	237	Kendal	100
Aberystwyth	273	Leeds	93
Barnstable	389	Lincoln	154
Birmingham	202	Liverpool	175
Brighton	350	London	285
Bristol	300	Maidstone	315
Cambridge	230	Middlesbrough	39
Cardiff	320	Northampton	220
Carlisle	57	Norwich	254
Carmarthen	325	Nottingham	160
Colchester	283	Oxford	255
Dorchester	382	Penzance	486
Dover	382	Perth	153
Edinburgh	108	Plymouth	415
Exeter	373	Preston	415
Fort William	241	Salisbury	319
Glasgow	152	Sheffield	134
Gloucester	265	Shrewsbury	216
Guildford	308	Southampton	321
Hereford	268	Stoke	193
Holyhead	267	Stranraer	161
Hull	142	Taunton	341
Inverness	268	York	87

Size Miscellany

* Baby - Marian Chapman was the world's smallest baby, born in South Shields in 1938 weighed ten oz, she died aged 44.

* Hoppings - held on the Town Moor Newcastle is believed to be the largest travelling fair in the world. Set up by the Temperance movement, traditionaly everyone gets soaked anyway.

* Metrocentre - the biggest out of town shopping centre in Europe and the first out of town complex in the UK.

* Motion Simulator Ride - the longest motion simulator ride in the world is at LIFE Interactive World.

* Reinforced Concrete - Malmaison Hotel, the former CWS warehouse is thought to be the oldest, large scale ferro-concrete building in the country.

* Big Geordie officially known as BE1550W was Western Europes biggest walking dragline excavator when it started work at Widdrington, near Morpeth. It was replaced by the Ace of Spades in 1993 which is 1,000 tonnes heavier, but had a bucket the same size.

Firsts & Oldest

* Boy Scout Camp - the first boy scout camp was held in 1908 west of Park Shields Farm at the foot of the south Tyne valley (the much publicised Brownsea Island camp was a trial camp).

* Dog Show - the Kennel Club's first dog show was held in Newcastle in 1859.

* Life Brigade - the first volunteer life brigade was formed in Tynemouth in 1864.

* Street Lighting - Mosley Street in 1811 was the first street to have gas lighting and in 1880 became the first street to be lit by electricity.

* Pivoting Bridge - the Gateshead Millennium Bridge is the first pivoting bridge of its kind in the world.

* South Shields Gazette is the UK's oldest provincial evening paper.

* Team Valley Trading Estate - the first government-sponsored trading estate in the world.

* Turbinia - the first boat in the world to be powered by a steam turbine engine.

Newcastle

* Newcastle Brown Ale - UK's biggest selling bottled beer with approaching 100, 000,000 a year

* Newcastle Disease - found in poultry

* Newcastle Glass - a style of goblet

* HMS Newcastle - 8 vessels have been given the title

* Newcastle - Motorcyle, NUT, the Newcastle upon Tyne motorcycle company started manufacturing in 1906

Northumberland

* Northumberland Arms

* Northumberland Bitter

* Northumberland College

* Northumberland County Council

* Northumberland (Duke of)

* Northumberland Fusiliers

* Northumberland National Park

* Northumberland Plate

* Northumberland Tartan (also known as Shepherds Tartan)

* Northumberland Wildlife Trust

Index